POETRY
AND
THE WORLD

Robert Pinsky

The Ecco Press · New York

CONCORDIA UNIVERSITY LIBRARY
PORTLAND, OR 97211

Copyright © 1988 by Robert Pinsky

ALL RIGHTS RESERVED

The Ecco Press

100 West Broad Street, Hopewell, NJ 08525

Published simultaneously in Canada by

Penguin Books Canada Ltd., Ontario

Printed in the United States of America

Designed by Bruce Campbell

FIRST PAPERBACK EDITION

Acknowledgments are made to the following periodicals in which earlier versions of the indicated essays appeared: *Antæus*, "Poetry and the World"; *Critical Inquiry,* "Responsibilities of the Poet" (The Joseph Warren Beach Lecture at the University of Minnesota); *Ironwood,* "George Oppen: The Undertaking"; *The New Republic,* "Seamus Heaney's Island," "Elizabeth Bishop's Complete Poems" and "Salt Water"; *The New York Times Book Review,* "Philip Larkin in Prose" and "Solidarity Days"; *Shenandoah,* "American Poetry and American Life" (The Jean and Arthur Glasgow Lectures at The Washington and Lee University); *Southern Review,* "T. S. Eliot: A Memoir"; *Threepenny Review,* "Poetry and Pleasure"; *TriQuarterly,* "Form and Freedom." "Some Passages of Isaiah" appeared in *Congregation: Contemporary Writers Read the Jewish Bible* (Harcourt Brace Jovanovich). "Salt Water" appeared in *Golden Gate Watershed* (Harcourt Brace Jovanovich).

Library of Congress Cataloging-in-Publication Data

Pinsky, Robert.
Poetry and the world/Robert Pinsky.
—1st ed.
p.   cm.
1. Books—Reviews.   2. Poetry.   I. Title.
PS3566.I54P6   1988
814'.54—dc19   88-4411   CIP
ISBN 0-88001-217-X (pbk.)

Publication of this book was made possible in part by a grant from the National Endowment for the Arts.

The text of this book is set in Bembo.

Contents

Foreword

Although the contents have been published separately in the course of ten years, this is intended to be a book on a subject. Its parts have been selected and recast, and most of them were written, with the idea in mind of poetry's relation to its great, shadowy social context: "the world."

My approach to the question has been not systematic, but a series of raids and occasions. Their arrangement here means to suggest a movement that alternates between the general and the specific, to arrive at the personal—beginning with the rather big, blank terms of the title essay and ending with the passage of Isaiah that I memorized for my Bar Mitzvah ceremony.

I thank those who invited me to give some of the essays in their first form as lectures, with a particular debt to the late Dave Evans of the Napa Poetry Conference. I am also grateful to the editors who supplied occasions.

I think I rely on help from friends and family more than most writers do. I thank mine for their suggestions, their readings and re-readings, their frankness and their encouragement.

R.P.

I

POETRY AND
THE WORLD

Poetry and the World

I

In this essay I want to consider "poetry" in its broadest definition, to include such forms as the short story; and to consider "the World" in a relatively narrow definition. I have in mind the world of worldliness: the social world, but more particularly the social world in its alternate glamour and squalor, its almost identical powers to divert us and to jade us. It is what Ben Jonson could embody by saying "the Court"; and indeed, in his great poem "To the World: A Farewell for a Gentlewoman, Virtuous and Noble," Jonson does seem to use "the World" as if it and "the Court" were synonymous.

To assert the existence of such a worldly world implies that there is also a different, distinct world which is other, a spiritual world. Poetry in English, with the dual, linked courtly and devotional traditions of its first great flowering, has often involved the problem of an orientation to these two worlds. I would like to use this topic as the occasion for talking about a wide, perhaps eccentric range of works. It has occurred to me that many of my favorite works, recent and historical, involve a bridge or space between the worldly and the spiritual. Poetry itself suggests such a dualism, related in ways I can't unravel. That is, the medium of words is social, yet it can also be the fabric of the most rarefied, introspective ideas; and the sensuousness of poetry is to give elegance and significance to the sounds that breath makes vibrating in the mouth and throat, animating by art those bodily noises of communication. In such ways poetry seems to have a special, enigmatic relation to the worldly world. On a more immediate level, it is worth inquiring into the role of the worldly in contemporary poems: what role does "the

A "craft lecture" to the Napa Poetry Conference, July 1982.

3

World" in this sense play in the new poem one is about to write
or to read?

The first example, however, is from the sixteenth century,
Thomas Campion's "Now Winter Nights Enlarge":

Now winter nights enlarge
The number of their hours,
And clouds their storms discharge
Upon the airy towers.
Let now the chimneys blaze
And cups o'erflow with wine;
Let well-tuned words amaze
With harmony divine!
Now yellow waxen lights
Shall wait on honey love
While youthful revels, masques and Courtly sights,
Sleep's leaden spells remove.

This time doth well dispense
With lovers' long discourse;
Much speech hath some defence,
Though beauty no remorse.
All do not all things well;
Some measures comely tread,
Some knotted riddles tell,
Some poems smoothly read.
The summer hath his joys,
And winter his delights;
Though love and all his pleasures are but toys
They shorten tedious nights.

The poem celebrates with the utmost relish the scenes and diver-
sions which it puts in their proper place. While it can seem superfi-
cially a charming song about hardly anything at all, it is about that
proper place, the idea of decorum. What is startling is that the stuffy
idea of decorum can be treated with such energy and ebullience, an
omnivorous verve that extends its appetite to flirtations, poems,
riddles, dance-steps, wine cups, the miniature honey-comb of lights
and the massive, fantastic storm.

Yvor Winters has used Campion's opening lines—"Now winter nights enlarge / The number of their hours"—as a *locus classicus* for the effective use of connotative or supra-rational effects in language: the word "enlarge" denotes rationally only the relative number of hours in a winter night, but its aura magnifies and enhances the large scale of the charming, almost Disneyesque storm and towers. In a similar vein, Winters points out the pleasing connotative harmony of "waxen lights" with "honey love": the castle with its comb of cells becomes a cozy, mysteriously sunny beehive in the thick of winter.

Such "harmony" and "amazement," to borrow Campion's own terms, are so egregious in the poem that Winters found them convenient examples of certain rhetorical effects. The harmony and amazement, blending the golden with the leaden, and blazing discharge of energy with well-tuned spells, by being made so prominent perform for us Campion's relation to these aristocratic, intoxicating worldly pastimes. The amazing, harmonious blending of air and architecture, wine and words, enlargement of space and time, rests on a sense of limit.

This idea of limit is quite explicit in the second stanza: the prolix, amoral rituals of courtship are limited by being assigned, with a smile, to the season of long, cold nights. And then, in a marvelous line, "All do not all things well": love-making, dancing, riddle-setting, the performance of poems—individuals are limited by their skills at these diversions; and the diversions themselves are limited, implicitly by their collocation and explicitly by the affectionate, but diminutive terms of the last two lines:

Though love and all his pleasures are but toys
They shorten tedious nights.

For a good poem to end with a brief summarizing moral statement violates a creative-writing slogan; but that is another example of the sense of limit on which Campion's song founds its success. It is a shrewd, oddly detached praise of both pleasure, and pleasure's limits.

II

Pleasure, especially the linked pleasures of art and sexual attraction, is the primary and perhaps the quintessential attraction of the worldly. In some of the stories of Isaac Babel, pleasure plays a central role in a fictional questioning of the worldly world, and its reality. Perhaps the odd comparison comes to mind because the idea of "the Court" persists in Babel, making possibly one of its last non-archaic appearances in literature. Needless to say, Campion's relation to "Courtly sights" is less complex than Babel's politically, and possibly in every other way, too. Though I will only gesture a little in the direction of such complexities, a brief attempt may suggest some comparative terms for the ways a contemporary poet stands in relation to the attractions and limits of the world.

In Babel's story "An Evening at the Empress's," the narrator is a hungry young poet, rather knowing and flippant in his narrative manner, drifting through the streets of Petersburg on a cold night in the early years of the Revolution:

> I needed a place to shelter. Hunger was plucking at me like a clumsy kid playing a fiddle. I went over in my mind all the apartments abandoned by the bourgeoisie. The great squat hulk of the Anichkov Palace heaved into my line of vision. That was the place for me.

He slips into the empty entry hall and through the uninhabited palace, to find himself in the private library of the Dowager Empress Maria Fyodorovna—the mother of the late Nicholas II, and born a Princess of the Danish Court. An old German, functionary under People's Commissar for Enlightenment Lunacharsky, is about to go to bed:

> My luck was really kissing me on the lips; I knew this German. I had once typed for him, free of charge, a declaration about his lost identity papers. He belonged to me with all his honest, sluggish guts. We decided that I had come to see Lunacharsky and was just waiting for him in the library.

I quote Max Hayward's translation (from *You Must Know Everything,* ed. Nathalie Babel), the tone of which one is inclined to trust, because this youthful, bohemian-wise-guy toughness of speech modulates into a poignant, important contrast.

After eating his rough ration bread from an ancient Chinese

lacquer table, while snow falls harshly on the granite city, the young writer takes down some of the Empress's books, on which a warm light falls in "lemon cascades." His response—the story's response —to these books has a peculiar, subtle flavor. I think that it touches upon the conflict between pleasure and time, the Court-World's splendor and the cruel limits imposed upon it by another world; the way Babel mingles nostalgia and irony seems to me like an effort to pin down those limits, to define the relation between the body's craving for comfort and ease on one side, and the cold truths of the soul on the other. The medium for all this is supplied by the elegant, pathetic old books:

> The books, their pages moldering and scented, carried me far away to Denmark. More than half a century ago they had been presented to the young princess as she set out from her small, sedate country for savage Russia. On the austere title pages, in three slanting lines of faded ink, were farewell good wishes from the ladies of the court who had brought her up . . . her tutors, parchment-faced professors from the Lycée; the King, her father, and her weeping mother, the Queen. On the long shelves were small, fat books with gold edges now gone dark, ink-stained children's Bibles with timid blots and awkward, homemade prayers to the Lord Jesus, small morocco-bound volumes of Lamartine and Chénier with withered flowers crumbling to dust. I turned over these thin pages, snatched from oblivion; the images of an unknown country, a succession of unusual days passed before me—low walls around the royal gardens, dew on the close-cropped lawns, sleepy emeralds of canals, and the tall King with chocolate-colored sideburns . . .

I think that this is no mere elegy, just as (on a different plane) Campion was not writing mere party-music.

One of the ways in which it is not mere elegy has to do with the context: the sudden, asbsurdly luxurious roosting place of the Revolutionary-era poet. His historical, political and cultural perspective allows him, in the next paragraph, to speak of the former Danish princess as "a small woman with powder worked into her skin, a shrewd schemer driven by a tireless urge to exercise authority, a fierce female among the Preobrazhensky Grenadiers, a merciless but attentive mother who met her match in the German woman"—that is, in her daughter-in-law the Czarina. The imaginative sympathy and amused judgment, the stylization and intimacy join other disparate elements of Babel's work, held together by his mysterious urgency of vision.

His work, in general, meditates the grace and energy of the actual world, and the horrible deficiency of order in the distribution of grace and energy. A brutal soldier, an exploitative regime, or imbecile fate itself, like a pig unwittingly gobbling a live chick or a pearl necklace, may be the vessels of the attractive force or elegance. The pleasure of the world is splattered about insanely, unpredictably, or embalmed in the dusty atmosphere of books.

Yet the stories, dramatizing this mess with their mingled appetite and horror, seem by their jangling of contexts to insist that a decorum, a limiting boundary, must prevail ultimately. I think that part of what makes Babel a great artist is that he does not glibly propose an ultimate order to be embodied merely by "art itself." On the contrary, there is something like the respectful but limiting tone of Campion's phrase "Some poems smoothly read," in the way the narrator's cockiness and the library's "ghosts with their bloodied heads"—the young artist and the old culture—chastise and expose one another. Neither of them feels quite as real as the relation between them, the historical violence and possibility that brings them strangely together.

This sense of limit and proportion emerging from violent disparities underlies the wry, anarchic grin of Babel's final sentence: "Let those who have fled it know," says the young man, who after recovering at the Palace sleeps the night in the train station, "that in Petersburg there are places where a homeless poet can spend an evening." The energy of the story centers not on the two places, nor even on the contrast between them, but on the changing Petersburg that brings them to the poet on a single night.

The lost, worldly pleasures of the Danish or Czarist court, and the crude worldly wants of the young poet whose luck kisses him on the lips, complement and negate one another: they are not all that there is. Somewhere in the narrative intelligence that encompasses both of these disproportionate realms is a value above them. This value is implicit, perhaps, in the fact that the back-currents of revolution have brought the young drifter to this room, and in the more remarkable, more absurd fact that he can read and respond to the pathetic books in the room. The last sentence is ironic and comic about the historical swirl that brings a half-frozen young scribbler to dine on coarse bread in a palace, and to sleep in a train station; but there is in the sentence, too, a kind of pride or pleasure, a need for things to work out in revolutionary Petersburg, and a germ of justification for that need.

That germ makes Babel's story more than an elegiac contrast of past and present worlds. Though one must call it political, it gives the story the spiritual force of a critique of both those worlds.

If we ask how the Campion song manages the balance needed to celebrate a world of elegant diversions and sexual pleasure, while confidently asserting the limits of such "toys," the answer would have to do with an implicit context. To avoid any embarrassing intellectual-historical clichés, let us say about the context simply that it is the kind of cultural and intellectual context on which such limits and judgments might rest. That is, Campion's imagined soirée implies a cultural frame in which worldly pleasures have their place within a distinct hierarchy. I think that in a more complex way, Babel's sense of balance in relation to the pleasures of the Anichkov Palace depends on a sense of another, higher, more stringent world. His willingness to be hopeful or exhilarated, in his strange historical moment, is as invisible and implicit as the Chain of Being (and so forth) in "Now Winter Nights Enlarge."

This idea of a kind of metaphysical political hope—or if not a hope, a sense of possibility, however desperate or ironic—embodies what I mean by another world. The idea's presence and importance in Babel's story are heightened, I think, by Babel's reworking of this same material in a later story, "The Road There" (as translated by Andrew R. MacAndrew). In this version, Babel can be said to turn up the volume of all elements: the poet is also a soldier, leaving the collapsed front of 1917 for the city. On the train, an idealistic Jewish schoolteacher and his young wife, carrying papers signed by Minister of Enlightenment Lunacharsky, fall asleep together "whispering about educational methods that would produce well-rounded citizens"; then, this couple become the victims of murderous brutality at the hands of a detachment of anti-Semitic peasants who check papers at a stop. The soldier–poet nearly has his frozen feet amputated, and spends some time in a hospital before getting to the Anichkov Palace. There, he not only eats, but is bathed, spends the night, is given the Czar's dressing gown and cigars by the official in charge, who is a former comrade-in-arms. The nostalgic, funereal elegy, going over "Nicholas II's toys . . . Bibles, volumes of Lamartine's poetry," is also expanded and intensified.

Though in some ways the story is less successful in this more explicit version, the idea of a beleaguered hope, expressing itself through the limits of the worldly, is more clear. "He's one of us," the old comrade announces, and the narrator is made a translator in the Commissariat.

> I set about translating the depositions made by various diplomats, *provocateurs,* and spies.
>
> Within a day, I had everything—clothes, food, work, and friends, friends loyal in life and in death, such as can be found in no other country but ours.
>
> That was how, thirteen years ago, my great life, full of ideas and joy, began.

The young Jewish schoolteacher on the train was shot in the mouth, his genitals cut off and pushed into the wife's mouth; the male nurse who bandaged the narrator's feet quoted Engels on the abolition of nations, but disagreed with Engels, asking the narrator in effect "What are you Jews after?" All of this material, narrated abruptly and without comment, heightens the irony in this final reference to "my great life"; but it also heightens the importance of the wish to believe that the loyalty, comfort, place in the world are true. The escape from history, though political in means, is for Babel unworldly and spiritual in its pained essence.

III

The elegance of the world, and its appalling cruelty, may be represented by the "harmony divine" of well-tuned words and the "savage Russia" of historical reality. Both elegance and cruelty are forced by the works of art to recede a certain amount into perspective. The pleasure of divine harmony is ultimately just a "toy"; the savagery of Russia is a fluid, violent amalgam of brutality and exalting possibility. In both poem and story, the social world, with its pleasures, limits, horrors, is put firmly in its place.

The pair of recent poems I have in mind might be said to proceed in the opposite direction, trying to locate the part of life that is not social, not of the World. These poems are the first two in Elizabeth Bishop's book *Geography III*. In a peculiar way, they recall Ben Jonson's poem, the Farewell "To the World" I alluded to at the outset. Jonson's noblewoman addresses the world:

> Do not once hope that thou canst tempt
>   A spirit so resolved to tread
> Upon thy throat, and live exempt
>   From all the nets that thou canst spread.
> I know thy forms are studied arts,
>   Thy subtle ways be narrow straits,
> Thy courtesy but sudden starts,
>   And what thou call'st thy gifts are baits.

The brilliant line about courtesy, and the one about forms, anticipate the later lines where this militant posture is pretty clearly directed toward the Court, as epitome of the World at its best and worst:

> Then, in a soil hast planted me
>   Where breathe the basest of thy fools;
> Where envious arts professed be,
>   And pride and ignorance the schools;
> Where nothing is examined, weighed
>   But as tis rumored, so believed;
> Where every freedom is betrayed,
>   And every goodness taxed or grieved.

The embattled contempt (superbly driven home by the rhymes) yields to a somewhat different, perhaps surprising variety of "scorn," tempering the conventional theme of *contemptus mundi* with a peculiar, almost sweet note of resignation:

> But what we're born for, we must bear:
>   Our frail condition, it is such
> That, what to all may happen here,
>   If it chance to me, I must not grutch;

Else I my state should much mistake
  To harbor a divided thought
From all my kind—that for my sake,
  There should a miracle be wrought.
No, I do know that I was born
  To age, misfortune, sickness, grief:
But I will bear them with that scorn
  As shall not need thy false relief.
Nor for my peace will I go far,
  As wanderers do, that still do roam,
But make my strengths, such as they are,
  Here in my bosom, and at home.

The military nobility of "resolved to tread / Upon thy throat" has become an equally stern, but more controlled, inward, even domestic kind of defiance: to "make my strengths, such as they are, / Here in my bosom, and at home." The words "I my state should much mistake / To harbor a divided thought / From all my kind" are especially affecting because they contradict the poem's inner direction and amend the "noble gentlewoman's" main response to the World. That response, her final moral resource, is isolation.

Isolation is a starting place and a central concern in Bishop's *Geography III*. The opening poem, "In the Waiting Room," portrays a seven-year-old child's realization that she is in a world of people and artifacts—and, even more terrifying, is a part of that world. That is, she is among the "grown-up people, / arctics and overcoats, / lamps and magazines," "Osa and Martin Johnson / dressed in riding breeches," "a dead man slung on a pole / —'Long Pig,' the caption said," "black naked women with necks / wound round and round with wire," the "shadowy gray knees" and "different pairs of hands /lying under the lamps"—all the grotesque, manifold contents of the *National Geographic* magazine or of the waiting room. But more, she is a member of that world, part of the contents, without having decided to be, and an all-but-anonymous part of the swirl:

I felt: you are an *I,*
you are an *Elizabeth,*
you are one of *them.*
Why should you be one too?

And:

> What similarities—
> boots, hands, the family voice
> I felt in my throat, or even
> the *National Geographic*
> and those awful hanging breasts—
> held us all together
> or made us all just one?
> How—I didn't know any
> word for it—how "unlikely" . . .
> How had I come to be here,
> like them . . .

It is hard to picture a more explicit, graphic version of a self needing to isolate itself from the social, worldly world, in order not to be lost in it. From the moment the child realizes this situation, a conflict begins. As the poem says: "The War was on."

"Crusoe in England" is (among other things) an allegory of the solitary, inner life in relation to the engulfing, numbing World. The poem's genius and originality stem partly from the moral insight that makes the solitary inner life something quite far from a paradise. It is an "other" world; and it is the object of affection (to be precise, of nostalgia)—but it is no heaven: "my poor old island," with its "fifty-two / miserable, small volcanoes," hissing, and its hissing turtles, "cloud-dump" sky, waterspouts, one kind of berry, goats. Taken as an allegorical self-portrait of one's inward life, it has the wit to be neither flattering nor flatteringly self-accusing. It is interesting, harsh, strange.

Correspondingly, the social world, the World itself, the other island of England to which the solitary has now returned, is not presented in trite or literary terms as sinister, monstrously huge, malevolently controlling, dramatically unjust. Rather, it is dwindling, numbing, rather cozy as well as depriving; it is where one lives if the sense of another, personal world has flagged:

> Now I live here, another island,
> that doesn't seem like one, but who decides?
> My blood was full of them; my brain

bred islands. But that archipelago
has petered out. I'm old.
I'm bored too, drinking my real tea,
surrounded by uninteresting lumber.
The knife there on the shelf—
it reeked of meaning, like a crucifix.
It lived. How many years did I
beg it, implore it, not to break?
I knew each nick and scratch by heart,
the bluish blade, the broken tip,
the lines of wood-grain on the handle . . .
Now it won't look at me at all.
The living soul has dribbled away.
My eyes rest on it and pass on.

In the conflict between the isolated world of the self and the communal world of England, the knife is a charmed artifact, a sacred weapon—but only in its primal context. On the terrain of the worldly, it becomes like a poem written years ago, when the World was not an enveloping, suffusing mass: when the maker was isolated from it.

That isolation is presented as onerous as well as sacred, an occasion for pathetic melancholy as well as for pride. Is it a matter of accomplishment, a matter, even, of volition? Bishop treats that question with a marvelous combination of comedy and cruelty:

I often gave way to self-pity.
"Do I deserve this? I suppose I must.
I wouldn't be here otherwise. Was there
a moment when I actually chose this?
I don't remember, but there could have been."
What's wrong with self-pity anyway?
With my legs dangling down familiarly
over a crater's edge, I told myself
"Pity should begin at home." So the more
pity I felt, the more I felt at home.

Her Crusoe questions whether the life apart from the World— the life of a castaway—is an imposed circumstance, or a product of the will. He does not directly raise the question of its value, but "pity" is only one of the products of his "island industries." He also creates home-brew, dreams, a philosophy, a parasol and trousers, a home-made flute, a baby goat dyed bright red with berry juice—suggesting that the world of isolation is the world of compulsive, sometimes trivial or frightful art-making. Crusoe's dancing, flute-playing, drinking, dressing-up constitute a kind of court-life of one. His nightmare is of other islands—other people and their own isolate, demanding, particular selves, each "an *I*" if not "an *Elizabeth.*" If self-pity begins at home, could sympathy ever extend to the grotesquely multiple other-worlds of humanity at large?

> I'd have
> nightmares of other islands
> stretching away from mine, infinities
> of islands, islands spawning islands,
> like frogs' eggs turning into polliwogs
> of islands, knowing that I had to live
> on each and every one, eventually,
> for ages, registering their flora,
> their fauna, their geography.

This idea of a kind of Christian love—"self-pity" extended as a principle of acceptance to the whole swarm of isolate souls—is too appalling. Better to settle for the aggregate island of England and the World, or to be grateful for the saving exception of Friday.

It seems to me that in its way "Crusoe in England" treads upon the throat of the mere World, treads too on the World's trite expectations about the other world, about the "inner life" in this case of "an artist." Nor does Bishop exactly "harbor a divided thought" from the rest of us. The "other islands" have their flora, fauna, geography; the author of this poem simply does not know anything about them, is made sick by the thought of needing to know about them. Compared to Campion's benign, confident categorizing of "love and all his pleasures" as "but toys" within a divine harmony, Bishop's other world of the isolated self, and the isolated, mortal relationship ("my dear Friday") seems rather a desert plant: harsh, sturdy, vigorous on minimal terms. Even Babel's version of the worldly pleasures and diversions of a lost court or a luxurious room is less severe than the almost monastic calm of Bishop's protagonist.

But what is inspiring to me in these poems by Bishop is the insistent, credible enactment of a human soul that is in the World, but not entirely of it, outside of the World, but not entirely apart from it. Her poems suggest that when we write, we need not be limited merely to the spinning-out of the filaments of memory and autobiography, on the one hand, or on the other hand merely to idly shifting the diverting kaleidoscope of imagination. Without neglecting the pleasures, interests, urgencies of the communal realm, she stays true to the way the mind itself craves something beyond that realm. And she does that without sanctifying either realm.

In fact, like Campion in his poem and Babel in his story, Bishop seems deliberately and explicitly to tease our easy responses about the holiness or specialness of art, especially in its relation to the World. The Court, nowadays, has been replaced as the repository of human elegance and creation by other official institutions: the archive, the performance center, the museum:

> The local museum's asked me to
> leave everything to them:
> the flute, the knife, the shrivelled shoes,
> my shedding goatskin trousers
> (moths have got in the fur),
> the parasol that took me such a time
> remembering the way the ribs should go.
> It still will work but, folded up,
> looks like a plucked and skinny fowl.
> How can anyone want such things?
> —And Friday, my dear Friday, died of measles
> seventeen years ago come March.

In Bishop's allegory of the World and the individual artist, the memorabilia and leftovers—not just the manuscripts and diaries and letters perhaps, but the work itself as well as the desk and materials —embody a pointless husk, the visible shell of a flown, invisible and intractable form of life.

Why do we want such things? How can anyone get pleasure from them? For the artist, the actual anniversary of a particular death may mean far more. But for the world, the comical, laborious parasol and the pathetic, decomposing goatskin trousers are charged with meaning and mysterious force. "All do not all things well." The gift of the makers, the ornament of skill, provides an elegant diversion from long nights, or from atrocities of history; and beyond that, it is a gift that suggests by its origin that there is another place than this one—though it be as small, hard and isolated as the island of a single soul.

The Collected Williams, Part One

Walt Whitman prophesied that the United States was too immense, unprecedented, strange and fragmented to be held together by anything but poetry. The American poet since Whitman whose work most wholeheartedly takes up that vision of poetry as a central national art is William Carlos Williams.

Today, more than a hundred years since his birth and nearly twenty-five years since his death, his poetry more than ever embodies the scope and freshness that go with such surviving, if threatened, ideals as democratic culture, modern art and the New World. Williams was an experimental artist in the generation that forced new perceptions of reality on the world—and he was also a medical doctor with a long, busy career in his home town of Rutherford, New Jersey. That is, he lived and worked at the center of American life, and also in the orbit of the radical avant-garde. Like no other American modernist, he knew the daily life, the speech and manners, of working-class, lower-middle-class and middle-class Americans. He knew the life of a town, a city and a region, and he brought some of the cool, arrogant detachment sometimes associated with his profession to that life. As a writer, he approached it and its physical setting with a kind of antagonistic relish, seeing his culture confidently from inside, yet from the unsettling angle of a great formal innovator and a severe critic. Because of this unique vision from within and without, Williams's art provides a continuing challenge. His influence has been immense, but his model has yet to be completely appreciated. In that sense, I think he is still an innovator, an artist whose work helps point toward the future.

For Williams, originality of technique and the ambition to write a poetry of American life, in language based on American idiom,

A review of *The Collected Poems of William Carlos Williams: Volume I, 1909–1939* (New Directions, 1986) edited by A. Walton Litz and Christopher MacGowan.

embodied a single, unified project. That unity of purpose is every-
where in this book. Williams wrote poems that were conscious
lessons by example in the making of free verse, in ways that were
at the same time a lesson in his kind of attention:

To a Poor Old Woman

munching a plum on
the street a paper bag
of them in her hand

They taste good to her
They taste good
to her. They taste
good to her

You can see it by
the way she gives herself
to the one half
sucked out in her hand

Comforted
a solace of ripe plums
seeming to fill the air
They taste good to her

The homely phrase "They taste good to her" moves through the
different emphases of its four repetitions as if Dr. Williams were
using a pointer or brilliant audio-visual aid to teach us all what lines
are, and why one would write in them.

That is, first we get the five-word phrase in its whole prosaic
form. Then the analytic effect of cadence and line cutting across the
sentence brings out the mysterious process of syntax, stressing first
the predicate adjective "good," then the verb "taste" with the
pronoun "they" as its subject (the word "plums" does not appear
until two stanzas later) and at the end of the stanza the isolated
phrase "good to her." When the repeated sentence comes back in
the last line, fitted entire into a line again, it is transformed. Rhythm
and repetition have brought back to life the force and elegance
inside a simple phrase.

But the restored process of language is only part of what the poem accomplishes. There are some plums, and a woman, and they taste good to her. The repetitions have a moral force, made explicit by the phrase "you can see it." The taking in of supposedly ordinary experience is Williams's great subject, and the energy lurking inside the adjective "good" or inside the syntax coursing through five monosyllables indicates the energy of the senses, a force so powerful that you can see it in another person. The almost hectoring repetition becomes a way of saying how simple such seeing is, and how difficult: if you pay attention, you can see the emotional shape enclosed in a phrase until it seems to fill the air. That is, you can see not merely a scene containing a character and some plums, but the process of the plums tasting good to her. If you pay sufficient attention, you may even devise a way to say it as plainly as you see it, making the most ordinary materials—"they taste good," a small child could say it, "poor old woman," it is what anyone might call her—memorable.

The example set by such poems sheds a harsh, impartial light over various kinds of contemporary taste in poetry. I mean, in one direction, the limp, rhythmless poems in short prosy lines that dribble down the pages of magazines, often a poetry based on the notation of observed details—and in another direction, forced, lurching, unidiomatic work in rhyme and more or less iambic meter, often a poetry of wit. Both modes, in relation to Williams's project, underestimate the multiple demands of experience and form, idiom and attention. I think that people tolerate such things because, though many like the idea of poetry, few hope to feel much excitement about a poem. The taut, syncopated movement of Williams's poem generates an excitement that reminds us what poems can do.

How can one define that movement? Williams's accomplishment has sometimes been confused with a kind of verbal photography, as if the point were to depict physical realities or visual impressions in words. But his famous slogan "(No ideas but in things)" was not "No ideas, but things." And in context, the phrase is not only bracketed by parentheses but surrounded by dynamic one-word sentences: "Compose." and "Invent!" The emphasis is on motion and energy, not depiction. He characteristically builds observation and "concrete" diction toward the attainment of an emotional process or idea, such as "solace": the apparent "abstraction" or directly named feeling that flowers out of all the careful attention given words for what can be seen, smelled and touched.

Swift movement between image and idea in the poems corresponds to the restless play among kinds of language: for example, between Latinate vocabulary and formal syntax (his careful subjunctives, or the occasional first-person "shall") on one side, and on the other plain American words and constructions. This movement, too, is both a formal principle and a thematic, even in a way a political, matter. The underlying conception of the United States as a source for the material, as well as the language, of poetry was no bland celebration of national life, nor was the Williams verbal style a mere wholesale, softening adaptation of colloquial language. His language is not the sentimental, static adaptation of American idiom of, say, Sandburg's "Chicago," but rather an ever-shifting, eclectic experiment in daring blends and savage, unexpected harmonies. Similarly, Williams presents an America that is provisional, still unmade, even terrifying in its rawness. "The pure products of America / go crazy," begins one of his most famous, and darkest, poems. Movement and speed, for good or ill, characterize both this vision of reality and the poet's stylistic response. He delighted in noting and discovering manners as a living flux, and around 1916 ended a poem ("The Young Housewife") with the lines

> The noiseless wheels of my car
> rush with a crackling sound over
> dried leaves as I bow and pass smiling,

observing the little nod we make with the steering wheel in our hands, the old European court gesture in its new vernacular setting: the car; the street; a thrilling, ruthless efficiency of motion; the self-consciously libidinous doctor looking at a young housewife at the curb, with similes for her in his head as he passes over the leaves in his heedlessly rushing contraption.

But description falls short of Williams's poems because the language he wrote in was like his conception of the country: not only provisional, but alertly inventing itself as it went. Thus, any simple alternation would be too mechanical for the exuberant, testy energy that delighted in pitching formality and high language against and into and around their supposed opposites, so resourcefully, with such cunning surface innocence, that high and low, formal and informal, cannot be told apart:

FINE WORK WITH PITCH AND COPPER

Now they are resting
in the fleckless light
separately in unison

like the sacks
of sifted stone stacked
regularly by twos

about the flat roof
ready after lunch
to be opened and strewn

The copper in eight
foot strips has been
beaten lengthwise

down the center at right
angles and lies ready
to edge the coping

One still chewing
picks up a copper strip
and runs his eye along it

This is entirely an account of the roofer's work and yet also of the work of the poet who runs his eye along the scene. The two stanzas about the beaten copper strips perform the trope of poetry delighting in its own difficulty of composition, like the lines in Yeats's "Adam's Curse" about how hard it is to write verse that sounds natural, or Ben Jonson's lines about revision in his elegy on Shakespeare. Without mentioning poetry or himself, or neglecting the roofers, Williams conveys all of this by implication, partly through combining disparate kinds of words. "Fleckless light" is elevated and poetic, whereas "separately in unison" is obsessively precise, and while "coping" and "eight foot strips" are technical in another way,

it is hard to say if "strewn" is archaic and high like "fleckless"—
or the most technical term of all, a part of the sweet old jargon of
the crafts and trades, and their techniques.

The gesture of picking up the stuff of work while still chewing,
like the bow while driving the car, makes a spontaneous, graceful
transition between formality and improvisation, necessity and plea-
sure. On their level, the gestures embody the fluid, inspired inven-
tion that was the poet's central aesthetic principle, and a kind of
ethical or political ideal as well. That ideal has something to do with
the way works of art imply who art belongs to, and the poetry in
this volume conveys that its radically fresh art belongs somehow to
us who live the actual American life Williams's poetry comes from,
and calls to account. It is as if he urges us to be both at home with
our materials, and "still chewing," impatient to transform them.

The early pages of this book trace the development of an indige-
nous American avant-garde style, a unique modernist accomplish-
ment that embraces all of the poet's intelligence along with all of
his American experience. That accomplishment should embody a
standard for any living American poet who sets out to write,
whether in elegant stanzas or jagged ones. From around 1914 on,
Williams's work attained an implied critique of our culture that still
penetrates in a special way because it comes from within, not from
the more European or global perspective of Pound and Eliot. By
bringing together his stringent idea of art and a transforming vision
into the ordinary, Williams by 1939 had set a continuing, essential
challenge for American readers and poets.

Philip Larkin in Prose

"I don't want to go around pretending to be me," says Philip Larkin at one point in this new prose collection, striking a note that recalls the sour, majestic refusals of his poetry. The paradoxical setting for this remark is a transcribed literary interview, a form whose very purpose is contrived self-presentation. Moreover, some of the brief prose works in the volume present a valid but artful self-portraiture, just as when Mr. Larkin is reluctantly having himself drawn out by the *Observer* or *Paris Review*.

By "me," he is entitled to mean quite a lot. Philip Larkin is one of the best living English poets, and one of the very few English contemporaries whose work has won deep admiration in America. That admiration is the more sincere if it is, for many American readers, a little grudging because Mr. Larkin can sometimes sound anti-American (as an important subcategory of anti-Abroad). He is also outspokenly anti-modernist in his approach to poetry, painting and music. His political views are distinctly non-progressive. Both his genius as a writer, and these opinions, are displayed in *Required Writing*.

Thus, Mr. Larkin's protest against public self-impersonation will not prevent readers from looking for him in his book. Those who love poems like "The Old Fools," "The Whitsun Weddings" and "Poetry of Departures" will value these prose pieces for what they say and what they are, but also as further evidence about who the poet is, or wants us to think he is.

As a critic, Mr. Larkin is nearly always lively, and often insightful. At his best, he writes an uncluttered, funny and sensitive prose that merits comparison with work by the commonsense poet-critics of our language, from Samuel Johnson through Yvor Winters and

A review of *Required Writing: Miscellaneous Pieces 1955–1982* (Farrar, Straus & Giroux, 1984) by Philip Larkin.

Randall Jarrell. At his worst, he strikes silly or repellent attitudes, suggesting a shallow attempt indeed to be himself.

On the level of the sentence, here is an example of Mr. Larkin using his cudgel fairly handily:

> Every poet's reputation fades in so far as his language becomes unfamiliar, and despite the iron lung of academic English teaching Marvell is no exception.

Here is an example, about the poetry of William Barnes, of Mr. Larkin at that difficult job, simple and balanced description:

> His view of nature is clear, detailed and shining, full of exquisite pictorial miniatures: his view of human life is perceptive, compassionate and sad.

As these examples suggest, the prose in *Required Writing* has many of the strengths of the poems: clarity, a sense of rhythm and assymetry, knowing how to time elements like "iron lung" or "sad," and a deflating, all but despairing defiance of cant. In the verse, this tone of nearly-giving-up is sometimes reflected formally by characteristic slant rhymes, loosened iambics, broken or brilliantly fudged rhyme schemes and patterns.

Such elements in Mr. Larkin's writing seem deeply connected to two qualities of English life that often strike visitors: vulgarity and coziness. In English speech, these qualities are reflected in the savage understatement and defensive gloom that Mr. Larkin has elevated to the lyric.

In his writing, the vulgar and the cozy often lead to a sense of life that is fresh, blunt and sad with an emotional penetration almost as great as his master Hardy's. At other times, what emerges is a mean provinciality. Occasionally, Mr. Larkin affects the voice of a bluff, genially philistine reactionary who dislikes "portraits with both eyes on the same side of the nose," and resents the destruction of "happy" jazz by "Negroes" who have gone to Juilliard. ("Who is Jorge Luis Borges?" "Oh I adore Mrs. Thatcher.")

This stylized, funny-papers version of himself seems to amuse Mr. Larkin, and through an odd turn of fashion it seems to amuse others, too. Perhaps it would be harmless, if it didn't make a superb poet

sound like a bar-bore, or an academic dinosaur clumsily baiting
junior faculty:

> It seems to me undeniable that up to this century literature used
> language in the way we all use it, painting represented what anyone
> with normal vision sees, and music was an affair of nice noises rather
> than nasty ones. The innovation of "modernism" in the arts con-
> sisted of doing the opposite.

This leering little act parodies the view of poetry Mr. Larkin puts
forward, a view that is simple, bluntly powerful and recklessly
circumscribed. Poems, he thinks, should give pleasure, preferably
immediate pleasure, to the "cash customers" whom he prefers
over "the humbler squad whose aim is not pleasure but self-
improvement." "Poetry," he says, "is an affair of sanity, of seeing
things as they are." On the one hand, the poet's job is to "re-create
the familiar," on the other, the poet's "business" is "externalizing
and eternalizing his own perceptions in unique and original verbal
form." Mr. Larkin opposes the "American, or Ford-car, view of
literature, which holds that every new poem somehow incorporates
all poems that have gone before it, and takes them a step further."
The modern, as embodied by Beckett, Pound, and at least some of
Joyce, yields only "mystification and outrage."

   This view has its limits. (Charlie Parker and Pablo Picasso are also
high on the Larkin hit list; he appears to consider Parker joyless and
Picasso unpopular and difficult!) But within these limits Mr. Larkin
writes movingly and illuminatingly about such topics as his work
as a librarian. He also writes wonderfully about Thomas Hardy,
Wilfred Owen, Stevie Smith, Ogden Nash, Barbara Pym, Anthony
Powell. Mr. Larkin casts a clear, cool eye on the post-1940 Auden,
and his very brief remarks on Housman and on Edward Thomas are
tantalizingly rich and suggestive.

   When he grounds himself firmly in the idea that "poetry, like
all art, is inextricably bound up with pleasure," Mr. Larkin is not
merely the clownish, complacent plain fellow who won't be tricked
by "modern art." His better self is a stubborn, brilliant conservative
critic who puts his faith in his powers, and in the human hunger
for art: "If sometimes I have failed, no marginal annotation will
help now. Henceforth, the poems belong to their readers, who will

in due course pass judgement by either forgetting or remembering them."

The two pieces on Hardy are especially good, based as they are on Mr. Larkin's own deep pleasure in his subject. "Hardy taught one to feel," he says in homage, and memorably evokes Hardy's abundance, his truth, and his sombre, copious music.

The most notable failure of enthusiasm in the book is Mr. Larkin's attempt to present American readers with the poems of John Betjeman, a comically unconvincing effort that is also highly revealing. He quotes the following four lines as an example of "command of detail" and the "glitter" of "sustained felicities":

> The lofty entrance hall, the flights of stairs,
> The huge expanse of sunny drawing room,
> Looking for miles across the chimney pots
> To spired St. Pancras and the dome of Paul's.

This is too dull for The Stuffed Owl, it is The Stuffed Sofa.

Even more remarkably, and damagingly, Mr. Larkin cites these lines admiringly as "social history":

> The girls, ambitious to begin their lives
> Serving in *Woolworth's* rather than as wives;
> The boys, who cannot yet escape the land,
> At driving tractors lend an awkward hand.
> An eight hour day for all, and more than three
> Of these are occupied with making tea
> And talking over what we all agree—
> Though "Music while you work" is now our wont,
> It's not so nice as "Music while you don't."

Mr. Larkin writes, "I find the last five lines not only a pertinent summary of a subject no other present-day British poet has tried to deal with, but singularly unforgettable."

The subject, visible under the plodding rhetoric and clumsy fitting of syntax to pentameter line, is the laziness and triviality of —to use a suitable period phrase—the lower social orders. Can it be that Mr. Larkin is so eager to endorse the attitude that he persuades himself the writing is "singularly unforgettable"?

Toughness and insularity have led Mr. Larkin to his best works, and to his worst. At this point one could draw the conclusion that in poetry he puts to the service of vision the very qualities that sometimes cloud his judgment in prose, and so forth.

But it is not that simple: for instance, in one of Mr. Larkin's poems a young American academic, portrayed making "the money sign" with his fingers, and committing a mistake in grammatical mood or number in each phrase he speaks, complains that he "wanted to teach school in Tel Aviv, / But Myra's folks . . . insisted I got tenure."

Incredibly, in *High Windows,* on the same pages as the unforgettable title poem and "Going, Going" and "The Old Fools," in one of only twenty-four poems, Mr. Larkin pauses to make this ignorant, rather stupid joke about Jews. It is spectacularly unworthy.

My point is not that poets must be sanitary liberals, or excellent people in all ways, but that Mr. Larkin's judgment is terrifically deficient in vital areas. And to separate judgment about life from literary judgment, either explicitly or by finding the meaner side of the Larkin persona merely amusing, something to overlook with a grin, would be to trivialize poetry.

My final example of this principle will be from Mr. Larkin's writing about jazz, and his attitude toward his beloved Louis Armstrong. Mr. Larkin finds jazz after the hot era—Coltrane, Davis, Gillespie, Monk, the Modern Jazz Quartet, Parker, Rollins, the works—*"ugly on purpose"* (his italics) and not the music of "happy men." He associates sophistication about harmony, composition, and the range of world music with the Juilliard generation of "the post-war Negro."

(I would expect Mr. Larkin to know about the classical training of many of his supposedly naive heroes: for instance, the fact that his example of the "happy" black musician, Fats Waller, studied advanced counterpoint with Leopold Godowski, and credited his complex left hand ability to Bach inventions.)

The sophistication of the younger generation, Mr. Larkin proposes, is essentially part of the larger modernist hoax, "to prevent people using their eyes and ears and understandings to report pleasure and discomfort," but he adds a social or political twist. "The tensions between artist and audience in jazz" (from which he says

art springs) "slackened when the Negro stopped wanting to enter-
tain the white man."

What is interesting about this theory is not the relatively inciden-
tal fact that it is drivel, or that it is unpleasant. Rather, what is worth
noting is the strange, ambiguous relation Mr. Larkin has to the early
jazz music he loves, and claims to love with an uncomplicated,
youthful joy. The mask of a hearty, charmingly feisty conservative
who just likes a tune "anyone" can hum and a verse "we all"
understand, falls apart.

It falls apart in the following quotation, from the very last
paragraph of *Required Writing:*

> In the great ironical takeover of western popular music by the
> American Negro (and remember the saying "Let me write a nation's
> songs, and anyone you like may write its laws"), Armstrong stands
> with Ellington and Waller as one of the Trojan Horses that brought
> it about. Mick Jagger at Altamont in 1969 is the logical outcome
> of Louis bringing the house down with "Ain't Misbehavin' " in
> 1929, and the process isn't finished yet.

Mr. Larkin's attitudes toward such matters as Jews, the poetry of
John Betjeman, jazz, American Blacks and modernism are important
only because they are his, because they help us to see the shape of
what he has done.

If Mr. Larkin, a superlative artist, prefers the third-rate verses of
Betjeman to the writing of Beckett, or if his love for Armstrong's
music is knotted up by a fear of the energy in that music, that is
his business. Ours, as his readers, is to understand both his best and
his worst impersonations of himself.

Poetry and Pleasure

In my teens, I memorized the following poem, without trying to memorize it, and without much thought for its meaning:

ON BEING ASKED FOR A WAR POEM

I think it better that in times like these
A poet's mouth be silent, for in truth
We have no gift to set a statesman right;
He has had enough of meddling who can please
A young girl in the indolence of her youth,
Or an old man upon a winter's night.

I think that what I liked about the poem was physical. That is, it had to do with what I could feel the consonants and vowels doing inside my mouth and in my ear.

About five years after I first read the poem, a teacher—a great teacher—upset me by criticizing the poem for its sentimental and anti-intellectual view of the nature of poetry. My teacher said that while one could not object to Yeats's refusing to write a poem to order on war or on any set subject, the reason Yeats gives is feeble, assigning poetry a trivial status:

[to] please
A young girl in the indolence of her youth,
Or an old man upon a winter's night.

This criticism, powerful and perhaps irrefutable though it is, ignores the historical attitude toward World War I of an Irish poet who a few years later would write "Easter 1916." It also ignores a loyalty

A "craft lecture" to the Berkeley Poetry Conference, July 1981.

I have never been able to shake off, toward the idea of pleasing and being pleased in works of art. Is my desire to make something capable of giving surprise, or giving a sensation of elegance, or a feeling of attraction—my desire to make something *pleasing*—simply a petty or irresponsible aspect of my strivings to make a work of art?

I think that the passion to give the gift of pleasure and interest, the desire to make this gift available (in theory) even to someone distracted by the body's sexual restlessness, or the body's need for comfort in cold weather, is an impersonal desire; Yeats's old man and young woman are not at a poetry reading, they are not book reviewers, he is not talking about their *response,* their compliments or their fan letters. He is talking about the idea of pleasing and interesting them, against odds, and without his even knowing it at the time. Though the poem may be subject to copyright law, and printed in a book that costs money, and though the concert and the museum too may cost money, there is another sense in which a work of art is a gift, a gift of pleasure which some of us aspire to give. (I borrow this idea from Lewis Hyde.)

Secondly, I want to say—as humbly as possible—that despite all the complexities of literary theory, for all the ingenuities of ambition or expectation, the trouble with most poems that fail—one's own poems, or poems written in workshops, or submitted to magazines, or published in books—may be described simply: they are not interesting enough to impart conviction. Most of them fail to be surprising or musical or revealing enough to arouse much interest; to read them, one must be a professional (and certainly not an indolent or drowsy professional). It sounds silly to say so, but some explicit sex, or a few jokes, or a bizarre personal confession, might make these poems more interesting. (It is true that such ingredients would not make them good poems; that is another reminder of how difficult it is to make a good poem.)

What we mean by feeling "interest," I think, is the free acceptance of the gift of pleasure. Without this component, however important the material in a work of art may be, or sophisticated its technique, we are responding with mere piety, or mere astonishment.

But is it possible to talk about how to be interesting, without sounding foolish? I will start with some rough categories for the kinds of interest I find in poems I love, and then cite some examples.

Poems, after all, are not the only compositions in words. Although poems are the most interesting kind of such composition to me, I can think of at least three others that please and interest most people, each having something in common with poems: songs, jokes and personal letters, which embody for me respectively the qualities of physical grace, lively social texture and inward revelation. Since good poems often have all three qualities, the examples I choose will be essentially arbitrary; in fact, I choose them partly to underscore the arbitrariness.

In the sixteenth and seventeenth centuries, poets wrote poems that have, to an amazingly pure degree, the interest of physical grace, the counterpoint of their music and their sentences. The physical transformation of words, simply by their arrangement, into something that approaches actual song, often gives an unexpected life, dignity and penetration to unpromising, formulaic subjects. Here is Ben Jonson singing the mating-song of an older lover, making his embarrassment about himself and his exaggerated appreciation of the person he loves into something that pleases me and cheers me up every time I read it:

> Let it not your wonder move,
> Less your laughter, that I love.
> Though I now write fifty years
> I have had, and have my peers;
> Poets, though divine, are men:
> Some have loved as old again.
> And it is not always Face,
> Clothes, or Fortune gives the grace;
> Or the feature, or the youth:
> But the Language, and the Truth,
> With the Ardor and the Passion,
> Gives the Lover weight, and fashion.
> If you then will read the Storie,
> First, prepare you to be Sorie
> That you never knew till now
> Either whom to love, or how:

But be glad, as soon with me,
When you know that this is she
Of whose beauty it was sung
She shall make the old man young,
Keep the middle age at stay,
And let nothing high decay
Till she be the reason why
All the world for love may die.

In a way, my point is that all good art defeats the predictable; Jonson defeats it with and through music: *with* music, for instance, in the way the most sing-song of all English meters is made fluent and personal and various by such means as his placement of the pause-within-the-line—now late in the line, now early:

Let it not your wonder move,
Less your laughter   that I love.
Though I now write fifty years,
I have had   and have my peers.
.   .   .   .
If you then will read the Storie,
First   prepare you to be Sorie
That you never knew till now
Either whom to love   or how.

But Jonson also defeats the predictable *through* music, because the elements that delight us appear to grow out of the swelling sense that he *will* sing, even though expectation and age threaten to hold him back. This resolve to sing keeps getting fuller and stronger: from the wry opening lines about faces, clothes, fortunes, then to the rhapsody about language, truth, ardor, passion, and finally on to the apotheosis of the beauty, and the appearance of the verb "to sing" itself—

Of whose beauty it was sung
She shall make the old man young,

—that follows; it is an elevated, victorious version of the opening lines in which the old lover protests that really, he is young. But who could predict:

Keep the middle age at stay,

Or, even more fresh and venturesome:

And let nothing high decay
Till she be the reason why
All the world for love may die.

That is, the traditional Petrarchan love-language of dying for the
personification of Beauty, seemingly immortal, is taken over for the
old lover's own purpose: both dying for love and being kept fresh
by it are epitomized by him.

Jonson's poem, then, pleases and interests because it is inventively
beautiful in sound, and because its beauty dramatizes the poem's
proposition that art can make fresh and heartening what would
otherwise be drab and discouraging. Though form has been looked
on sometimes as the most public, least personal part of poetry, here
form is an individual, physical expression of impatience with the
clumsy boundary of what is expected.

As a physical expression, in other words, the attractive form of
Jonson's poem is personal, the way one's way of dancing or gestur-
ing or walking is personal. Insofar as this is true, Jonson's achieve-
ment of a personal expressive rhythm, within a confining but
distinctly forceful meter, is horribly enviable for anyone who has
tried to put sensuous life and individual force into metered or
unmetered lines.

Part of the effect is not simply metrical, but springs from the
freshness and naturalness of idiom: "though I now write fifty years";
"poets, though divine, are men"; "it is not always Face, Clothes, or
Fortune"; "you never knew till now"; "be glad"; "this is she." These
phrases are Jonson's plain English, as fresh in their historical context
as the plain American of Williams, and when they coincide with
the measure there is the thrill of sensing that the rhythmic demands
of song and the nature of actual speech have been made to coincide,
as when a song's pattern and song-lyrics seem made for one another.

Finally, it's worth observing that the particular pattern of Jon-
son's poem seems especially well suited to the theme that skill can
elevate and transform an old, inert, provincial or discouraged body.
The pattern is "beheaded" tetrameter, which by dropping the first,

unstressed syllable that begins a normal tetrameter line emphasizes
the separation of the lines, most of them beginning, as well as
ordinarily ending, with a stressed syllable. Then, with a feeling of
exuberant transformation, the poet glides things back together by
flowing the grammar over that separation; Jonson's last lines might
have inspired Yeats in "Under Ben Bulben":

> Irish poets, learn your trade,
> Sing whatever is well made,
> Scorn the sort now growing up
> All out of shape from toe to top.

The note of exultation and scorn—in Jonson's lines, scorn for those
who put the body above the arts that animate it, in Yeats's lines,
scorn for those who fail to master those arts—in both poems re-
solves itself into a note of triumph. The sense of victory, of over-
coming the shapelessness or fatigue of the body, is near the center
of the pleasure of song. By fitting the grunts and vocalizations of
language into elegant, expressive patterns, poetry conveys a similar
pleasure in the human body as it apparently excels itself.

As to jokes, it is not their funniness that interests me in relation
to poetry, nor is it their structure, which is the aspect of jokes most
often taken up when speaking of poetry (as when a Shakespeare
sonnet is said to rely too much upon the weak punch line of its
couplet). To make it clear that I am not talking about jokelike,
funny elements in poems I will try to pick a fairly solemn poem,
with no particular punch-line structure, for an example of the
principles I do have in mind. These principles concern the alert
social texture of successful jokes, and in relation to that texture their
sense of context and power to generate context.

I think that the idea of "good jokes" and "bad" ones reflects a
misconception; the timing and social placement of the joke, and the
textural pleasures of its telling, matter far more than the mechanical
burning of a narrative fuse toward the little explosion of a punch
line. The joke about the one-armed piccolo player might be right
for a certain moment after a picnic, but not for the car-ride home.
Or the badness or bad taste of one joke might sometimes be more
successful than the seeming excellence of another. People naive

about jokes fail to see this enormously social, contextual limitation to the form, and are bewildered when the Jewish parrot joke that caused tears in one setting evokes only polite smiles in a slightly different one; moreover, such a teller exaggerates the importance of "how" it was told, while underestimating the original teller's sense of precisely when to time the joke.

Also, charm of texture probably matters more, compared to punch lines, than rhetorically naive conceptions of the joke assume: the way the woman who told the parrot joke hunched her shoulders and used head, rather than arm, gestures to suggest the parrot pointing out the *talis* it would like the tailor to copy for it in miniature; the way the woman pronounces or mispronounces *talis;* the way the tailor is presented as mixing the teller's idiom ludicrously with the ethnic idiom—touches like these, as they establish context and conviction, make up the living body of a tiny work of art, for which the punch line is merely the graceful closure. These touches are the expressive social gestures which in a poem we sometimes call "taste" or "timing" or "tact" or "wit."

I am afraid that I'll seem to be diddling with superficial matters that insult the serious and vital art of poetry; but I am trying to edge toward the altar of the mystery, by analogy—and the fleeting, social conviction and alertness that come to life when one person contrives a funny story for others resemble one aspect of the more enduring, freestanding conviction of the successful gift that is a poem. Moreover, this aspect of poems seems to me to be the one that criticism sees least clearly, and is most likely to mangle or bungle inadvertently.

If music conveys physical grace, this contextual alertness conveys a feeling of actual life at its best, of social liveliness. In the joke this liveliness is ephemeral and contingent. In the poem, it is the enduring generosity and subtlety of a human presence:

Piano

Softly, in the dusk, a woman is singing to me;
Taking me back down the vista of years, till I see
A child sitting under the piano, in the boom of the tingling strings
And pressing the small, poised feet of a mother who smiles as
she sings.

In spite of myself, the insidious mastery of song
Betrays me back, till the heart of me weeps to belong
To the old Sunday evenings at home, with winter outside
And hymns in the cozy parlor, the tinkling piano our guide.

So now it is vain for the singer to burst into clamour
With the great black piano appassionato. The glamour
Of childish days is upon me, my manhood is cast
Down in the flood of remembrance, I weep like a child for the past.

D. II. Lawrence modulates the presence of the human voice telling
this poem, whose subject—boy versus man, nostalgia versus passion,
music versus thought, "manhood" versus "softness," remembrance
versus the present, the human voice versus its accompanying "great
black piano" of feeling—is a stock source for poems, as mothers-in-
law or airplanes with ethnically various passengers are stock sources
for jokes. The modulation of the personal presence in the poem is
the source of its formal invention, its ability to pierce us with
something fresh, and not stock.

At the very beginning, the conventional "Softly, in the dusk" and
"Taking me back" tell us where we are, in the way that in the joke
form "a man goes to a doctor" or "a guy goes into a bar and says"
tell us where we are. The quasi-social convention tells us that
"child" denotes the same person as the adult who is being sung to,
and the vivid, nonconventional language—

A child sitting under the piano, in the boom of the tingling strings
And pressing the small, poised feet of a mother who smiles as
she sings.

—tells us that the energy is going to be in the past: the softness of
the dusk in the present, and the "boom of the tingling strings" in
the past. And though the "insidious mastery of song" is in the
present, it "betrays [him] back" to the past. The words "insidious"
and "betrays" put a steely spring into the social component of the
poem, the amazing spring of Lawrence's combative, moralistic side.

In relation to the social component of the poem, I want to return
to the idea of tact, or social judgment. There are two large ways

in which the poem seems related to society: sexually, there is a feeling made out of the Oedipal situation of the child, the infantilizing impact this has on the man, and the suggestion of male impotence; politically, the "cozy parlor" and the Sunday evening hymns place the memory in a certain religious, cultural and social strand of English life. But how pathetically wooden and imprecise my summarizing language is for the actual, pleasingly deft accuracy with which Lawrence's poem indicates these parts of what he has to say, including the contrast between the Baptist family home of the child and the elegant situation of the grown man. My lament at the clumsiness of my own definition, here, is a standard critical maneuver; but I think that criticism, despite such outward laments, tends to neglect the way that such matters of nuance and degree are not merely difficulties presented to the professional reader, and not even mere beauties of technique that make the work of art more to be prized; rather, the ability to introduce feelings and meanings to precise degrees, with compact, rapid accuracy, is at the core of the work of art. Such calibrations embody the way a work of art struggles for a claim on our attention. I think that this power is in a way a social grace or art—like the ability to time and present a funny story. (Needless to say, the sexual or sociopolitical matters at stake here may be considerably more demanding than the contexts I suggested above for the joke.)

But as poets (rather than readers) our concerns are different. One problem we may have in writing a poem is how to arrange and dispose a feeling—how to put something first, something else second, and so forth. The silliest joke, too, must solve this problem. Lawrence solves the problem in terms of a kind of narrative combat, I have suggested, between resistance and nostalgia, present and past, soft language and hard. In a joke, the comparable elements might be the ordinary and the preposterous, as in the countless stories in which a man goes into a bar with a polar bear, or a horse, or an invisible dwarf, or a mermaid. The skill (or art, if we choose) of presenting the joke is in presenting the dance or tension of the two elements, ordinary and bizarre. In Lawrence's poem, the dance or struggle I have indicated is dramatized by the rhyming, personal voice telling what happens, as it includes the opposed meanings of "cozy" and "insidious," the opposed roots and social contexts of those words, and the opposed social analogues of the rhetorical "great black piano appassionato" and the bare, plain "weep like a child":

> In spite of myself, the insidious mastery of song
> Betrays me back, till the heart of me weeps to belong
> To the old Sunday evenings at home, with winter outside
> And hymns in the cozy parlor, the tinkling piano our guide.

> So now it is vain for the singer to burst into clamour
> With the great black piano appassionato. The glamour
> Of childish days is upon me, my manhood is cast
> Down in the flood of remembrance, I weep like a child for the past.

There is something like wit—not mere wittiness, but social wit, an alert brilliance about tone, that calls up our own delight in nuance, our delight in not being stupid or bored—in the "glamour of childish days," the singer in clamor and the great black piano appassionato, piano and singer impotent to compete with the tear-flooded past they have called up. That language has literary and sexual implications—"glamour" and "childish" and "manhood cast down"—touched on so surely and unheavyhandedly that we are flattered, or anyway invited along pleasingly. The same can be said of the way "the old Sunday evenings at home" and "the heart of me weeps to belong" evoke, without mocking, a lower-middle-class elegance of speech.

If the poem's structure has anything like a punch line or final revelation, it is syntactical: after sentences and parts of sentences all beginning with modifiers, the last sentence links three strong substantive subjects that begin its three clauses—"glamour," "manhood," "I":

> the glamour
> Of childish days is upon me, my manhood is cast
> Down in the flood of remembrance, I weep like a child for the past.

We are given this by the teller to appreciate, like a sudden colloquialism or gesture by one telling a joke, and I think we appreciate it partly for the way he has created a social context for us and exploited that context. In other words, the three strong substantives please the reader not just formally, but as the capstone of a plot, involving the sexual and socio-economic matters I have (a bit ponderously) outlined. We respond to this social grace and penetration, or rather to this artistic imitation of social grace and penetration, with the pleasure of being taken out of ourselves, and yet also further into ourselves.

Finally, putting Lawrence's poem aside, I want to say again that I am not talking about the narrative element in jokes and poems, but about something communal in the art of presentation. Since I can't show you someone telling a joke, cast your mind to the Gable character and the Colbert character in *It Happened One Night,* when early in their flirtation, in order to fool some detectives, they improvise an argument in which they pretend to be a rather stupid married couple screaming at one another. It is a little work of art the two characters have made, and given to one another, and it is based on social understanding and imagination; and it functions— far more importantly than fooling detectives—to advance their sexual trust and respect. When Lawrence invites us to hear conventional and fresh language, coziness and insidiousness, when he has the child "press" rather than, say, "touch" the mother's feet—he is inviting us to take a pleasure like that of the two characters, based on a similar part of our intelligence, a similar wish to appreciate other people and their sense of themselves in their words.

If music's grace is the most basic aspect of a poem's appeal, and lively contextual sense is a poem's necessary social component, perhaps the most profound pleasure by which a poem engages our interest is by revealing to us the inward motion of another mind and soul. I associate this power with letters because I have found it impossible to write a good personal letter without going at least a little further into myself than I might in conversation; the element of planning or composition seems to strip away barriers, props and disguises, rather than to create them. I think we all find this true in letters from friends—even the brief hurried note seems to have concentrated some distillate of a person's inner nature. And to read an old letter of one's own is, sometimes, to be amazed at how revelatory the mix of news, musing, inquiry turns out to be. And as surely as the abstract yet physical course of music pleases us, or the skillful weave of telling in a social context pleases us, the revelation of an inward self pleases us.

One poet above all others has trusted this principle, has ruthlessly followed the assumption that what is in him, if he can only follow its tides and creatures as faithfully as a naturalist, will be beautiful and interesting. In this, I find Whitman to be just as he says he is, however calculating and programmatic he may be in other ways. His amazing poem "Spontaneous Me," for instance, presents a kind of deliberate sexual manifesto, with details far more pointed than what the poem calls "the negligent list of one after another as I happen to call them to me or think of them"; but on the other hand this alleged "negligence" is an accurate reflection of the poem's charm and force, which come from opening a kind of door into Walt. The idea of linking sexual energy and poetry, carried to absurd or sexist or self-important extremes, takes on the integrity that belongs to any actual single personality:

> The real poems (what we call poems being merely pictures,)
> The poems of the privacy of night, and of men like me,
> This poem drooping shy and unseen that I always carry, and
>   that all men carry.

The self-consciousness of the letter-writer, who is naked in the sense that he is stripped of the cloaking effects supplied by physical presence, social presence, often leads the writer to comment, as Whitman does here, on what he is writing.

But this self-reflection is perhaps more external, less revealing, than the series of set-pieces or rhetorical ebulliences that succeed it. And most revealing of all is the movement from one rhetorical flourish to the next. The letter-writer types in apparently random order a series of paragraphs, news, inquiry, anecdotes, asides, complaints, boasts, apologies; and as a whole, the plot created by the paragraphs reflects the characteristic energy by which the writer's personality moves. And as "Spontaneous Me" moves from the hilariously pornographic encounter between "the hairy wild bee" and the "full-grown lady flower" whom he grips with "amorous firm legs" as he "hankers up and down" and "takes his will of her," on to the wet woods, then to the two sleepers "one with an arm slanting down across and below the waist of the other," then hastily to the "smell of apples" and sage, and so forth, leaping with a slightly nervous, elated grin from the erotic to the innocent, the generalized to the personal—the balletic jumps come to seem even more important and heartfelt than the places they touch.

Of course, these inventive loops and plunges and changes of manner are partly a technical feat, alert to what the reader will demand once the title "Spontaneous Me" has been linked to the sexual material. The poem surprises by going on, and then on, and varying catalogue against tender description, alternating shouted lists and whispered descriptions. But leaving technical considerations aside, consider the beautiful passage on masturbation, and the sequence that follows it:

> The limpid liquid within the young man,
> The vex'd corrosion so pensive and so painful,
> The torment, the irritable tide that will not be at rest,
> The like of the same I feel, the like of the same in others,
> The young man that flushes and flushes, and the young woman
>   that flushes and flushes,
> The young man that wakes deep at night, the hot hand seeking to
>   repress what would master him,
> The mystic amorous night, the strange half-welcome pangs, visions,
>   sweats,
> The pulse pounding through palms and trembling encircling
>   fingers, the young man all color'd, red, ashamed, angry;
> The souse upon me of my lover the sea, as I lie willing and naked,
> The merriment of twin babes that crawl over the grass in the sun,
>   the mother never turning her vigilant eyes from them,
> The walnut trunk, the walnut husks, and the ripening or ripen'd
>   long-round walnuts,
> The continence of vegetables, birds, animals,
> The consequent meanness of me should I skulk or find myself
>   indecent, while birds and animals never once skulk or
>   find themselves indecent.

The last five lines embody what I mean by the revelation of self through movement from one thing to the next. On the one hand,

on the surface, they present a Whitmanian doctrine about the inno-
cence of sexuality, with the line where he lies willing and naked
under the souse of his lover the sea at the fulcrum. (That line is the
most daringly explicit in one way, and draws a seemly veil of "the
natural" over things, in another way.) On the other hand, the
working out in texture of the "red, ashamed, angry" youth, to the
souse of the sea, to the twin babes is full of invention and
peculiarity; we can feel his affected, excessive, unerring brain
stretching for inspired examples and finding them. This seems par-
ticularly true of the mother "never turning her vigilant eyes" from
the twin babes—a Victorian contrivance of sweetness that is also the
maternal poet (or reader) refusing to avert watchful eyes from what
two people may like to do together. And then walnuts, of all things,
and of all the attributes of birds, animals and vegetables (!), their
"continence." The odd little association of sound between that word
and "consequence" is part of the persuasive psychological fabric. It
helps make the poem seem the easy going-into oneself of

> Beautiful dripping fragments, the negligent list of
>   one after another as I happen to call them to me
>   or think of them,

while the sequence of examples for innocence and passion, anxious
to persuade and calm the reader, reminds us how planned and
determined the poem is. This dual sense of a freed, wandering mind
in the writer and his extreme consciousness of the reader, the combi-
nation of nakedness and a rather specific awareness of audience, gives
Whitman's structure its energy, more than selfhood or doctrine
could do alone. The subtlety of this movement, more free than
conversation and yet more contrived, less formal than discursive
prose and yet more concentrated, resembles the best kind of letter.

What impresses me about the Whitman poem—about all of the
poems I have discussed—is the fact that its essential appeal cannot
be attributed to the way it fulfills certain (undeniably valuable)
standards that pervade creative writing or literary criticism, as they
approach poetry. Vivid phrases; striking images; sharp physical de-
tails; beautiful, quotable language; important ideas (philosophical,
political, psychological): no one could deny that these elements are
important, and that they contribute to our desire to read Whitman's

poem, Lawrence's, Jonson's, our pleasurable assent to *be* reading them. But if gorgeous, impressive language and profound, crucial ideas were all that poetry offered to engage us, would it seem—as it does to many of us—as necessary as food? Would eloquence and truth, by themselves, be enough to compete with (say) the movies, for our attention?

As I re-read the passage in "Spontaneous Me" about masturbation, shame, innocence, exuberance, pleasure, freedom, identity, and search in it for the three qualities I have tried to consider as essential, I find them at the center of the charm and passionate engagement I find in the passage. In the sounds of a line (the rapid beginning and slow ending of the phrase "merriment of twin babes," the consonants in "merriment" and "twin"; the consonants and vowels in "grass," "crawl," "mother," "never," "vigilant") there is something comparable to the tune you hear and want to hum, and hum again. In the teasing alternation of preacherly and pornographic phrases, there is something comparable to the bright, socially observant talker's sense of audience and social context, evoking, mocking and confessing to the prudery and lasciviousness of his time and place. And in the way the structure, avowedly random and ostensibly determined by its political and psychological ideas, conveys the moral drama of Whitman's mind as it moves through its examples and assertions, there is something comparable to the pleasure given by a letter taken out to be read again, because it embodies a considerable soul in action.

This movement—physical in the sounds of a poem, moral in its relation to the society implied by language, and the person who utters the poem—is near the heart of poetry's mysterious appeal, for me. Such movement cannot be affected or faked. It comes from conviction: confidence in the power of rhythm; trust in the social generosity between artist and audience; belief in the movement of one's own thoughts and feelings. Convincing movement is what commands interest. (Boredom appears to be a response to the tunelessness, timidity or weak faith that are in the work of art, a sense that the soul is standing still.)

I'd like to close with a poem that seems to me to present such movement in a rather naked form, Czeslaw Milosz's "Incantation." It is also a very encouraging poem on the subject of poetry. Rather than apologize for the fact that it is a translation, I'll suggest that it all the more presents the essential movement or conviction I'm trying to get at, and all the more may risk violating standards of poetry we may take from the terms of creative writing or book reviews. With those terms uppermost in our mind, would we have the boldness to write the first line of this poem? Its first three lines, or its first six?

INCANTATION

Human reason is beautiful and invincible.
No bars, no barbed wire, no pulping of books,
No sentence of banishment can prevail against it.
It establishes the universal ideas in language,
And guides our hand so we write Truth and Justice
With capital letters, lie and oppression with small.
It puts what should be above things as they are,
Is an enemy of despair and a friend of hope.
It does not know Jew from Greek or slave from master,
Giving us the estate of the world to manage.
It saves austere and transparent phrases
From the filthy discord of tortured words.
It says that everything is new under the sun,
Opens the congealed fist of the past.
Beautiful and very young are Philo-Sophia
And poetry, her ally in the service of the good.
As late as yesterday Nature celebrated their birth,
The news was brought to the mountains by a unicorn and an echo.
Their friendship will be glorious, their time has no limit.
Their enemies have delivered themselves to destruction.

It is good to read a poem that suggests that poems are supremely important, and that many good poems remain to be written. The art, says Milosz, is young; and it is the friend of truth. That is, it promises surprises far beyond the clichés of fine writing or self-regard, with the appeal neither of an easy cosmetic rhetoric nor of a secret code that ignores the reader and the world; it promises vital, unsuppressible knowledge. The creation of interest through the most pleasurable ways of knowing: that is what poetry—the fascinating, more physically graceful friend of Philo-Sophia—is. Or anyway, by entertaining such a definition of poetry, as the creation of an interest in truth through pleasure, Yeats's poem about the ambition to please may be a little redeemed.

Marianne Moore: Idiom and Idiosyncracy

Marianne Moore's poems have a social presence, you might even say a sociable presence. That presence is distinct from Moore's tiresome public caricature as a genteel, fey, impishly brilliant old lady in a peculiar hat—and yet gentility and idiosyncracy are unquestionably part of the true social presence in the poems. Like many stereotypes, this is one we can neither quite feel comfortable with, nor altogether reject. In Moore's best work, the outer force of manners penetrates beyond a charming or complacent gentility, to become a profound moral force, as in the great novelists; and the inner force of idiosyncracy becomes the sign of a passionate, obdurate selfhood. I think that to understand the peculiar strengths or limitations of this poet, we have to look at her work in the light of such matters as the relation of language and poetry to social life and even to social class. These matters seem all the more important because Moore was a modernist, one of the generation of poets that raised anew questions about the kind of poetry that might be suitable for an American and democratic culture.

Partly because of our own social habits and predispositions, we readers often respond to Moore's work in social terms: people dote on her poems, or find them annoying, a little as if responding directly to a person and her remarks. Here is a very slight but relevant early poem that presents itself explicitly as a social action. The poem (omitted from the *Complete Poems* of 1967) has the pleasing title "To Be Liked By You Would Be a Calamity." It begins with a quotation from Thomas Hardy:

"Attack is more piquant than concord," but when
   You tell me frankly that you would like to feel
      My flesh beneath your feet,
         I'm all abroad; I can but put my weapon up, and
      Bow you out.

Gesticulation—it is half the language.
　　Let unsheathed gesticulation be the steel
　　　　Your courtesy must meet,
　　　　　　Since in your hearing words are mute, which to my
　　　　　　　　senses
　　　　　　　　Are a shout.

One thing this little epigram demonstrates is that Moore can write in the mode of colloquy without writing colloquially. That is, address and something like exchange take place, but not vocally, and not in words much like any conversational language of twentieth-century America: the words "I can but put my weapon up, and / Bow you out" represent part of an exchange, but an exchange imagined in the terms of another century. Like the deliberately period metaphor of swordplay, the "steel" that is "unsheathed" and "put . . . up," this period voice is a defensive and offensive weapon, a way to keep anger and hatred at some distance while striking at them. Even "My flesh beneath your feet," because of "flesh," is a bit stagy and unreal. The most spare, "natural" language and the most memorable phrase coincide on the phrase "Gesticulation—it is half the language." And that moment in the poem is the most clearly inward: self-addressed, not directed toward the imagined interlocutor at all. The poem is indeed about conversation that does not take place, words that are withheld, language as a social weapon that goes unused except in Moore's powerful imagination.

The artificiality, in other words, is the point. We can picture the actual gesture with which Moore politely and hostilely bowed someone out of her office—personally, I believe such a moment did actually happen—but the address is not only highly, but pointedly, artificial, an invention that represents its underlying true action of silence or reserve. She creates an artificial dialogue to dramatize, and to protect, her inward poise. The poem attains a feeling of social superiority through artifice and the weapon of refusal, the submerged sharklike intelligence that conceives both the unsheathed steel of gesticulation and the "put up" weapon of actual speech. The poem is in short an elaborate way of saying, "I am not speaking to you"—or more accurately, "I am not speaking to that person."

Repeatedly and characteristically, Moore's poems construct an elaborate social presence that contrives to disguise or protect, just as manners sometimes do in life. Moore's ambivalent attraction toward the idea of communal life expresses itself, then teasingly cancels itself, characteristically, in a conversation that is not conversation. Reticence and withdrawal, as in "To Be Liked By You Would Be a Calamity," often underlie apparent engagement. Moore's two most characteristic rhetorical modes, apostrophe and quotation, amount to a kind of parody, or at least a blatantly artificial reconstruction, of discourse between people.

In this mock-colloquy, her quotations invoke the possibility of heeding the voice of another, while the poet contrives to manipulate and assign meanings. And in the other direction, her apostrophes often invoke the possibility of addressing another only to suggest the unreality of such address. In *Observations,* there are poems grammatically addressed to an intramural rat, to a chameleon, to a prize bird who is G. B. Shaw, to the sun, to Disraeli, to military progress, to a steamroller, to a snail, to George Moore, to Molière, to the ibis as statecraft embalmed, to a pedantic literalist, to the son of the author of a history book, to critics and connoisseurs, to one by whom it would be a calamity to be liked, to Ireland and to roses. In none of these poems does the second-person pronoun have the kind of reality it has in poems like, say, Yeats's "Adam's Curse" or Bishop's "Letter to N.Y."

The unreality of the second person is skillfully exploited in some of these poems, often with comic effect, and often aggressively. In "Critics and Connoisseurs," the polysyllabic, first-person sentences describing the swan are artfully contrasted with an abrupt, monosyllabic turn toward the one addressed, "I have seen you":

I remember a swan under the willows in Oxford,
    with flamingo-colored, maple-
        leaf like feet. It reconnoitered like a battle-
ship. Disbelief and conscious fastidiousness were
        ingredients in its
            disinclination to move. Finally its hardihood was
                not proof against its
            proclivity to more fully appraise such bits
                of food as the stream

> bore counter to it; it made away with what I gave it
> to eat. I have seen this swan and
> I have seen you; I have seen ambition without
> understanding in a variety of forms.

This is very shrewd writing. The sentence "It reconnoitered like a battleship," while itself terse and plain, introduces the comically ponderous quality that the next sentences embody, "its hardihood was not proof against its proclivity," and "such bits of food as the stream bore counter to it," and so forth, a deadpan irony of inflation, just a little as if mouthed by Robert Morley. By contrast it gives the cutting social edge to "I have seen this swan and I have seen you."

There are many contrasts at work here: polysyllabic abstract moral terms played against the brilliantly observed, specific feet of the swan; the first person against the second person; sentences like Latin played against sentences like abrupt speech; abrupt compression played against unexpected flourishes of elaboration. All of these are part of the larger contest between idiom, Moore's acute and rather satirical sense of a communal speech, and idiosyncracy, her equally sharp sense of language as the weapon of her private self which observes the swan and the ant, the critic and the connoisseur. She addresses herself to these objects of attention, and also addresses them grammatically, in a formal way—but not actually, not socially, or even anything like it. You might call these two poems "mock satires," in that they present personal, inward meditations in the outward form of a social clash.

Idiom is the sameness of the language customarily used by people in a particular place. Idiosyncracy, with its first half from the same root, is in language the sameness of a particular person's *crasis,* or constitution. Considering these two elements as partially opposed is a way to understand the dry, skeptical reservations, the rock-hard mistrusts, that stand behind some of Moore's relatively warm-looking, humanistic passages.

The opening stanza of "The Steeple-Jack" illustrates the double quality I mean:

> Dürer would have seen a reason for living
> in a town like this, with eight stranded whales

to look at; with the sweet air coming into your house
on a fine day, from water etched
    with waves as formal as the scales
on a fish.

The line-ending emphasizes the phrase "reason for living" in isola-
tion: a kind of sardonic undertone that emphasizes, not habitation
("living in this town"), but a reason to stay alive. Dürer would have
seen a reason for living; do you, or I? Especially in a town like this?
That undertone of laconic desperation is not farfetched, since an
ocean turbulence affects both the actual stars and their religious
representation:

whirlwind fife-and-drum of the storm bends the salt
    marsh grass, disturbs stars in the sky and the
star on the steeple; it is a privilege to see so
much confusion.

"Confusion" is followed by an extended, hyperbolically long cata-
logue of flowers, a profuse list so eclectic and long that it is dizzy-
ing, even inchoate, and becomes bilious, imaginary, "not-right,"
animal, before it is punctuated at the end by an apparent apothegm
of small-town virtue:

             Disguised by what
    might seem the opposite, the sea-
side flowers and

trees are favored by the fog so that you have
    the tropics at first hand: the trumpet vine,
foxglove, giant snapdragon, a salpiglossis that has
spots and stripes; morning-glories, gourds,
    or moon-vines trained on fishing twine
at the back door:

cattails, flags, blueberries and spiderwort,
    striped grass, lichens, sunflowers, asters, daisies—
yellow and crab-claw ragged sailors with green bracts—toad-plant,

petunias, ferns, pink lilies, blue
    ones, tigers; poppies; black sweet-peas.
The climate

is not right for the banyan, frangipani, or
    jack-fruit trees; or for exotic serpent
life. Ring lizard and snakeskin for the foot, if you see fit;
but here they've cats, not cobras, to
    keep down the rats. The diffident
little newt

with white pin-dots on black horizontal spaced-
    out bands lives here; yet there is nothing that
ambition can buy or take away.

This garden is brilliantly disturbed, with its nasty-sounding "salpi-
glossis that has / spots and stripes." The bravura gaudiness and excess
of lines like "yellow and crab-claw ragged sailors with green bracts
—toad-plant" establish the mood of a centerless, sinister profusion
even before a stanza begins with the words "is not right," and the
establishment in the homely Eden of a domestic, unspectacular,
apparently even innocuous serpent.

But serpent the diffident little newt is, though not "exotic" or
tropical. At the apparent climax of an undecipherable abundance,
the serpent is there, "yet there is nothing that / ambition can buy
or take away." This is the tone and language of a plain, morally
stringent provincial sufficiency and calm, but like the opening lines
about seeing a reason to live, this Spartan formula has an ironic
undertow: the town's garden profusion as rich as the tropics offers
nothing that can be used outside of it. Ambition is either enclosed
within this place and its terms, or frustrated. Nothing is for export.
The student, in the poem's next sentence, sits with his "not-native
books" and watches the boats as they progress "white and rigid as
if in / a groove."

In this bleached, rigid, self-contained place, economy of gesture
governs flux and turbulence, as in a woodcut or engraving. Seagulls
rise around the clock or lighthouse without moving their wings—
a slight quiver of the body. Even the storm that disturbs the stars
in the sky and the star on the steeple does not shake or transform
anything; rather, it provides a significant spectacle: "it is a privilege

to see so / much confusion." Turbulence without change, abundance without harvest, elegance without bravado, and character without discourse or incident: it is a community, but one in which Moore's characters do not touch or address one another. The president repays the sin-driven senators by not thinking about them, and the college student with his books sees across a long perspective, as in the background of a Dürer woodcut, the central figure of the steeple-jack, who "might be part of a novel," but for us, is not.

The steeple-jack, the title figure in the first poem in Moore's *Complete Poems,* embodies the poet's relation to social or community life. He is not exactly isolated from the town: he serves the town by gilding its paramount symbol, and he also has posted two signs, one in black and white announcing his name and profession, and one in red and white that says "Danger." The steeple-jack is both prominent—he wears scarlet, he has a bold sign, he is high above—and also a small, attenuated figure, letting down his rope as a spider spins a thread. In his remoteness which is a measure of his courage, he resembles other figures, vulnerable and potentially lonely, who have in common their difference from the ambitious and gregarious. The stanza begins with the word "Danger," but the town offers relative safety for those who live with risk and rely on an inward reserve:

> This would be a fit haven for
> waifs, children, animals, prisoners,
>   and presidents who have repaid
> sin driven
>
> senators by not thinking about them.

Relative safety is a governing ideal in Moore's haven. Those who are as Moore says "each in his way" at home here—the hero, the student, the steeple-jack—live familiarly with the risk of failure. They are at home with that risk, and with countervailing hope, and thus they strive, provisionally. Manners, compared to morals, are more or less by definition provisional, and "The Steeple-Jack" is a poem powerfully, subtly contrived to construct a model of the world of manners, our communal arrangement.

Here, the gap between Moore's personal utterance and the shared language of idiom serves to make the emotion all the stronger. In this secular world, the poet's voice mediates between the ordinary and the mysterious. It is a voice sometimes informal, yet never quite demotic; it is non-judgmental, yet couched in the grammatical terms of the moralist: what "would be fit" or "is not right" or "what might seem" or "if you see fit." Her formal inventions bracket a capitalized "Danger" between stanza-break and period, or stretch over line and stanza a phrase—"the pitch / of the church // spire, not true"—defining the boundary between secular imperfection and religious hope, or between the provisional and the absolute:

> Liking an elegance of which
> the source is not bravado, he knows by heart the antique
> sugar-bowl shaped summer-house of
> interlacing slats, and the pitch
> of the church
>
> spire, not true, from which a man in scarlet lets
> down a rope as a spider spins a thread.

Because this figure puts out his danger-signs, "It could not be dangerous to be living / in a town like this." Up on the untrue spire gilding the solid-pointed star which on a steeple stands for hope, the steeple-jack is an artist at home in the town without being precisely in it. He leaves his laconic words of identification and warning behind, and puts the possibly deceptive gilding on the representation of a possibly justified communal hope. Though his very name, Poole, means a shared aggregate, and though he performs a communal service in a spectacularly visible way, he also embodies solitude and remove.

The aggressive mock-satire of "Critics and Connoisseurs" and "To Be Liked By You Would Be a Calamity" enact a highly artificial, almost parodic version of social discourse. They deal with fury and incomprehension: "ambition without understanding" in the first poem, and in the second words which to the person addressed are "mute, [but] which to my senses / Are a shout." The fury in "The Steeple-Jack" has been transformed into "the whirl-wind fife-and-drum" of a storm that disturbs, but remains highly localized—though something like repressed anger courses through the ambiguities about reasons to live, the thwarting of ambition, the untrue pitch and the double-edged standing for hope. The incomprehension or distance between people, the motivating force of the earlier colloquy-poems, has become part of Moore's peculiarly allegorized, but enigmatic, town. This brilliant invention, freighted with symbolic meanings but resolutely particular, down to its proper names, "Ambrose," "C. J. Poole," supplies a way for the poet to be present and emphatic, yet elusive. It allows her language to be familiar and sociable, yet never bound by the idiomatic. She has imagined a quiet, communal haven for idiosyncracy, and put it at the beginning of her complete poems.

Marianne Moore touches on the question of idiom in her *Paris Review* interview with Donald Hall. She begins with admiration for a stage play she has seen:

> The accuracy of the vernacular! That's the kind of thing I am interested in, am always taking down little local expressions and accents. I think I should be in some philological operation or enterprise, am really much interested in dialect and intonations. I scarcely think of any that comes into my so-called poems at all.

This is an elaborately complicated response, a maze of false and genuine modesty. However, the description of her poems as reflecting hardly any of the vernacular is basically true. In her next response to the interviewer, Moore talks of taking as an elective at Bryn Mawr a course called, remarkably, "seventeenth-century imitative writing—Fuller, Hooker, Bacon, Bishop Andrewes and others." One thing that animates the language of "The Steeple-Jack" is the way it takes us into her imagined place without being the language of a place. Moore's language in its full power is not what she calls "the vernacular"—has little to do with the speech of a place, much less of the streets; rather her poetic medium is partly a reflection of the ruminative, capacious discourse of seventeenth-century prose, and partly an assertion of the freedom of her own, autocratic *crasis*.

When Moore does reflect the speech of an actual American group or place, it is with an effect of conceivably deliberate distortion, getting things so thoroughly wrong that we wonder nervously if that is the point. That embarrassment is generated, for example, by her poem on the Brooklyn Dodgers, recklessly calling Duke Snider "Round-tripper Duke" or writing of teammates: "Ralph Branca has Preacher Roe's number; recall?" Whether deliberately or not, the mangling of baseball jargon, on one level comical, on another defines the gap between the shared language of the community and the separated, no matter how benign, utterance of the poet, isolated above.

That isolation has many corollaries, and invites speculation. From a viewpoint to do with social class, a strong drama of Moore's work is her effort to accommodate democracy, her egalitarian and patriotic American side, with what seems the unavoidable gentility of her language. This is a matter of manners that shades into politics, but in a complex way. Moore would be incapable of writing as convincingly "spoken" a passage as Bishop's, from *Manuelzinho:*

> You paint—heaven knows why—
> the outside of the crown
> and brim of your straw hat.
> Perhaps to reflect the sun?
> Or perhaps when you were small,
> your mother said, "Manuelzinho,
> one thing: be sure you always
> paint your straw hat."

That "one thing" with its colon is not part of Moore's range. Because it is part of Bishop's range, she can write this passage in a poem about a woman and her servant or dependent, a passage and poem that some readers have found condescending and cruel, and that some have found deeply understanding and humane. Either way, Bishop is in a theater of operations, a social place, that Moore does not enter.

From a feminist perspective, Moore's declining to reproduce something like the social art of conversation in her poems, even parodying that art by an autocratic system of apostrophe and quotation, is a way of refusing the realm traditionally or stereotypically assigned to women of intelligence and force: polite conversation, the little room in which Jane Austen's heroines must exercise their wills. There is another sense in which Moore is, in Sandra Gilbert's cogent phrase, a "female female impersonator," exaggerating and exposing expectations related to gender. The refusal of assigned terms characterizes some of her most memorable lines cast in the feminine grammatical gender, from "The Paper Nautilus":

> For authorities whose hopes
> are shaped by mercenaries?
> Writers entrapped by
> teatime fame and by
> commuters' comforts? Not for these
> the paper nautilus
> constructs her thin glass shell.
>
> Giving her perishable
> souvenir of hope, a dull
> white outside and smooth-
> edged inner surface
> glossy as the sea, the watchful
> maker of it guards it
> day and night, she scarcely
>
> eats until the eggs are hatched.
> Buried eight-fold in her eight
> arms, for she is in
> a sense a devil-
> fish, her glass rams-horn-cradled freight
> is hid but is not crushed.

"Hid but . . . not crushed": this treasured, painstakingly insulated "freight" is not merely the kernel of emotion at the center of the poet's art, it seems to be the accomplished burden of her personality itself. What gives emotional power to the images of protection and nurturing, what gives the "souvenir of hope" its dignity, is the way courage is evoked by images of transparency, delicacy, the "dull white outside." All of these images, because they evoke the nautilus's shell from its outward border, foreshadow the action of the eggs as new life coming out and away from it, to "free it when they are freed." The papery shell is compared to a "fortress," but a fortress less strong itself than the idea of "love," the "only fortress / strong enough to trust to."

This resolution would be sentimental in any poet less fortress-like than Marianne Moore. The amply dramatized isolation and remove, constituted in large part by the idiosyncratic, quasi-archaic, quasi-colloquial turns of word and syntax, all combine to give dignity and penetration to the idea of a shell opening trustfully in love. Depth of protective reserve and the gesture of opening inform the image in the last stanza of "The Paper Nautilus": the white-on-white grooves, "close- // laid Ionic chiton-folds" left in the shell when the eight arms have relaxed their watchful protective embrace.

This is the characteristic action of language and feeling in Moore, and it is a particularly complex or indirect one. Broadly speaking, one can think of poets as having characteristic turns of energy: Dickinson pitting wonder against despair; Yeats fitting together what has been broken; Williams peeling back integuments. The limitations of such quick tags are obvious, and yet it helps me to find the source of feeling in Moore's work if I think of her as constructing, exposing and disassembling an elaborate fortress. The materials of the fortress are idiosyncrasy and manners, manners of speech and the social manners they reflect. The town of "The Steeple-Jack," which is referred to as a "haven," does not present actual, kinetic manners between people, but it is depicted in sentences that tease and yearn toward idiomatic speech, then away from it. The town itself is like a newly-painted set, ready for the play of social life to commence, with its church columns of stone "made modester by white-wash," and:

> The
> place has a school-house, a post-office in a
> store, fish-houses, hen-houses, a three-masted
> schooner on
> the stocks.

The town, which contains one figure alone with books on a hillside and another isolated above, is as if poised for the ordinary activities of communal life, below its star which stands for hope—the same quality as in the paper nautilus's "perishable souvenir of hope."

Hope for what? Among other things, hope for the give and take of life, which in both poems is presented as if just about to begin. In the phrase from Henry James that ends Moore's poem on New York, "accessibility to experience." This action of declining a fortress, and welcoming experience, is profoundly moving. The staircase-wit of the mock-satires with which I began consign social experience to a kind of eternal previousness, addressed from behind the walls of idiosyncracy. In fuller poems like "The Paper Nautilus" and "The Steeple-Jack," a protected and protective shell frees and is freed, a "fit haven" is imagined in a moment of anticipation. Even the poem "Marriage" can be read as a dialectic between the two ideas of that enterprise as a form that contains, and as a form that mediates.

The idea of a shell that is first constructed, then disassembled, freeing what was inside and becoming free of it, provides a way of seeing Moore's work. We do not merely identify Marianne Moore by her protective shell of peculiarities, but value her for them. She is not one of those writers about whom we can say she is best when she is least idiosyncratically herself. Utterly to prize her idiosyncracy would be condescension, and yet to suppress or disregard it would be to reject an essential action of her poetry and the moral energy that drives her work. Overcoming or mastering a social manner that intervenes between the person and "accessibility to experience" provides a central drama in that work.

From one perspective, this drama has to do with a determined, persistent movement toward the demotic and the democratic, cutting against the genteel elements in Moore's idiom. From another, it is the drama of a woman artist alternately refusing and parodying both of the alternate social stereotypes: female charm and male assertion. From the biographical viewpoint, Moore's work reaches outward from the circumstances of her family. The father's insanity and absence, beginning before Moore's birth, left a kind of three-person social fortress: the mutual protection of a religious, middle-class family, economically insecure and socially exposed by the absence of the traditional patriarchal head. Dealing with that perpetual deprivation, and that immense embarrassment, gave the truncated family a delicately hardened protective architecture.

The visible forces in Moore's work are peculiarity and generalization, reticence and asseveration, and in language the eccentricity of the scholar and the central idiom of the marketplace. These forces bring together what is closed, like a shell or a provincial town, and the open seas of experience. Her evocation of these forces merits, and meets, the standard for art Moore proposes in the concluding line of "When I Buy Pictures":

It must acknowledge the spiritual forces which have made it.

This acknowledgment is exactly parallel to the shell's beautiful ionic grooves, the aftermark of a measured, protective pressure that has been relaxed. In language, the line enacts its proposition: to *"acknowledge* the spiritual forces that have made it." The verb "to acknowledge" is subtly and appropriately social, it implies an other: one acknowledges a gift, a compliment, an obligation. That is, social forces acknowledge spiritual forces, in their own terms, and thereby take on spiritual power. What Moore depicts, at her best, is the solitary and laborious approach to that attainment: the trek, you might say, through knowledge to acknowledgment. The sudden, even unexpected penetrations of emotion in Moore's work flare up from the tireless pressure of the poet negotiating and considering between her own way of talking and our way of talking, between discourse and discourse's imaginary re-making, the suspended life of a town and that life's forever hoped-for resumption. These oppositions embody the shared, socially visible quality of peculiarity that shadows the peculiarity of each distinct human soul.

Elizabeth Bishop's Complete Poems

The eery clarity and brilliant surfaces of Elizabeth Bishop's work have always been easy to see. Her first book, *North and South* (1946), contained poems that have been widely memorized, imitated, turned to as antidotes for slackness, and anthologized: "The Imaginary Iceberg," "Wading at Wellfleet," "The Man-Moth," "The Monument," "Florida," "Roosters" and "The Fish" are among these early poems—not bad for a first book.

But though the achievement and reputation increased with the publication of *A Cold Spring* (1955, Pulitzer Prize), *Questions of Travel* (1965) and *Complete Poems* (1969, National Book Award), the whole force and unique daring of Bishop's poetry may not have been quite entirely visible until her last book before her death in 1979, *Geography III* (1976). In the light of that book, all of her work seemed to change. The poet who might have seemed lapidary and self-effacing emerged as a radical explorer of selfhood's very nature.

Now, *The Complete Poems 1927–1979*, including translations, uncollected poems, juvenilia and occasional verses as well as a small number of new poems, shows the magnitude of this immensely readable, yet somehow oblique and elusive poet. It is an exciting, challenging lifework. Within her limitations—she was not prolific, she lacks boldness of scale—Bishop is original without the obvious rhetorical noises that sometimes pass for profundity.

Bishop is a lyric poet of solipsism yearning toward love, of metaphysical doubt acknowledging worldly charm and variety. But her isolated self is too proud to strut; and her doubt is too gravely absolute for heroic or Whitmanian manners. On the rare occasions when she reaches for the high style, the grandeur is based on a

A review of *The Complete Poems 1927–1979* (Farrar, Straus & Giroux, 1984) by Elizabeth Bishop.

negative assertion, as in the conclusion of "At the Fishhouses,"
where the water is

> Cold dark deep and absolutely clear,
> element bearable to no mortal.

The negative assertion, moreover, is tempered by the provisional
counterpoint of supposition and simile, an effect which further
qualifies the sublime, limiting how much can be known even of the
familiar:

> I have seen it over and over, the same sea, the same,
> slightly, indifferently swinging above the stones,
> icily free above the stones,
> above the stones and then the world.
> If you should dip your hand in,
> your wrist would ache immediately,
> your bones would begin to ache and your hand would burn
> as if the water were a transmutation of fire
> that feeds on stones and burns with a dark gray flame.
> If you tasted it, it would first taste bitter,
> then briny, then surely burn your tongue.
> It is like what we imagine knowledge to be:
> dark, salt, clear, moving, utterly free,
> drawn from the cold hard mouth
> of the world, derived from the rocky breasts
> forever, flowing and drawn, and since
> our knowledge is historical, flowing and flown.

It is *like* what we *imagine* knowledge to be. The simile and (as Jane
Shore has shown) the qualifying adverb ("then *surely* your tongue")
are hallmarks of Bishop's style and outlook. She reminds us that she
is making or positing connections between separate things, so that
we may even notice the idea of "mediation" in the hypothetical
"immediate" ache of the wrist. A steady fury with the very idea of
falsehood leads her to make every connection explicitly an inven-
tion, and her own invention. That a person can be known, or the
intensely visible world understood, is always left partly in doubt.
    Thus, the poet of gaiety and reticence also denies—all but arro-

gantly—that one person is likely to know another, or indeed that one particle of experience is more than provisionally linked to any other: "Everything only connected by 'and' and 'and.'" The line is from "Over 2,000 Illustrations and a Complete Concordance," whose travellers to the Holy Land and elsewhere witness a dazzling, sinister catalogue of contingent sights: Collegians "like ants" marching through St. Peter's Square, the juke box that went on playing "Ay Jalisco," the beautiful poppies splitting the mosaics at Volubilis, where "the fat old guide made eyes," the "little pockmarked prostitutes" of Marrakesh who "flung themselves / naked and giggling against our knees, / asking for cigarettes." Then:

> it was somewhere near there
> I saw what frightened me most of all:
> A holy grave, not looking particularly holy,
> one of a group under a keyhole-arched stone baldaquin
> open to every wind from the pink desert.
> An open, gritty marble trough, carved solid
> with exhortation, yellowed
> as scattered cattle-teeth;
> half-filled with dust, not even the dust
> of the poor prophet paynim who once lay there.
> In a smart burnoose Khadour looked on amused.
>
> Everything only connected by "and" and "and."
> Open the book. (The gilt rubs off the edges
> of the pages and pollinates the fingertips.)
> Open the heavy book. Why couldn't we have seen
> this old Nativity, while we were at it?
> —the dark ajar, the rocks breaking with light,
> an undisturbed, unbreathing flame,
> colorless, sparkles on straw,
> and, lulled within, a family with pets,
> —and looked and looked our infant sight away.

The nightmare of the dust-filled grave is not merely of death, nor even of nothingness, but rather of meaningless, accumulated particles, casually tangent. The clear sight that witnesses these separate particles cannot see the mysterious, meaningful and capitalized birth, nor can it "look itself away." The use of "infant" in its original sense—"unable to speak"—precisely underscores how incapable mere sight truly is: it can record only those tangent particulars. That is why the hesitation of simile concedes a harsher, more strictly limited truth than the magical blatant confidence of metaphor. Simile, unlike metaphor, makes the concession that no resemblance is absolute.

Nothing is more conventional in modern poetry than the valuing of metaphor above simile. The stark, unostentatious way Bishop's work reverses that convention is characteristic; she is too sure and proud to explain or to show off—partly because what she is sure of is the limitation, as of simile. The reader is free to misunderstand, or not, but italicizing rhetoric or self-explication will not be provided. Similarly, it is possible to make the false assumption that she describes the separate parts of the world, the sensory particulars, out of love for those physical details. But in fact, *The Complete Poems 1927–1979* records at least as much rage as love toward that merely visible, carefully recorded array of distinct things. That is, for all the pleasure of the eye, the poet's drama also includes the mind separating itself from the sensible world that nearly drowns the individual—as in the dizziness of "In the Waiting Room"—and the mind separates itself by seeing and naming all that is not itself. The extraordinary power of sight yearns to "look itself away." Each acute observation or similitude that the self makes as it regards the world is also a defiant, negative definition of one's own boundaries.

In *Geography III,* the separate self is associated with the figure of the island. The speaker of "Crusoe in England" has the nightmare of imagining all the other separate imaginations, each isolated subjectivity demanding the impossible, to be known:

> I'd have
> nightmares of other islands
> stretching away from mine, infinities
> of islands, islands spawning islands,
> like frogs' eggs turning into polliwogs
> of islands, knowing that I had to live
> on each and every one, eventually,
> for ages, registering their flora,
> their fauna, their geography.

Along with the other allegorized geographical feature of the volcano—the essential Bishop totem, molten rock pushed up from under the seemingly still surface—islands embody something in the poet's nature that is not merely pessimistic and enclosed, but antisocial: the lines preceding the ones I've quoted narrate Crusoe's dream of slitting a baby's throat.

If the reticence of simile and the isolated, volcanic island suggest Bishop's philosophical orientation, her social person is represented by quite different aspects of her writing. She is also a love poet ("Casabianca," "Chemin de Fer," "Insomnia," "One Art") and a poet of funny, charitable social comedy ("Filling Station," "Manners," "Letter to N.Y.," "House Guest," "12 O'Clock News"). Yet the poems often give a mysterious glamour and sweetness to the ordinary and domestic (the almost Norman Rockwell quality of people saying goodbye at a bus-stop while "a collie supervises"), in a way that suggests a feeling of being ineffably an outsider, a tourist from some other star, in relation to the banal customs of middle-class life. (Helen Vendler has described the poet's rapid, sensitive oscillation between "the domestic and the otherworldly.")

The feeling is expressed by the eye that notices, amid the bleached, salt landscape of "The Moose," the woman who "shakes a tablecloth / out after supper," and by the many times when language is allowed to pour bizarrely over the quotidian: the man in "Cape Breton," for example, who climbs a stile, carrying a baby, and crosses a meadow to "his invisible house by the water." Sometimes this is largely an effect of sound, rather than diction, as in the line (quoted earlier) "In a smart burnoose Khadour looked on amused," where having three iambic words with similar vowels coincide with three iambic feet, two of them adjacent, produces a reggae-like effect of reverse syncopation. Sometimes the effect is of diction and sound both:

The giant with the stammer
was the landlady's son,
grumbling on the stairs
over an old grammar.

He was morose,
but she was cheerful.

The bedroom was cold,
the feather bed close.

 ("A Summer's Dream")

Her last published poem, "Sonnet," conveys this aura of the familiar transfigured, in its conceits: the bubble in the spirit level, the caught needle wobbling in the compass, the freed mercury running from the broken thermometer, "the rainbow bird" of light cast flying by the bevel of a—characteristically—empty mirror.

The peculiar nature of Bishop's version of a Romantic theme— the self isolated in a world unlike it—was clarified by *Geography III*. That book might be described as the autobiographical writing of a non-autobiographical writer; it hovers near personal account without entering the terrain of memoir (much less "confession") for very long. Yet it is entirely intimate and inward. Reviewing the book in *The New Republic,* Harold Bloom wrote:

> Of her own generation of poets, which included Roethke, Lowell, Berryman and Jarrell, Bishop alone seems beyond dispute. As contemporaries, we may over-esteem the others, but Bishop's art is as unmistakable in its authority as the poetry of Wallace Stevens and Marianne Moore demonstrated itself to be, at an earlier time.

The Complete Poems 1927–1979 confirms this judgment.

Bloom's context for comparison raises another thought. Recent biographies of Delmore Schwartz and Lowell, and Eileen Simpson's *Poets in Their Youth,* call attention to the stereotype of the flamboyant, hungering, competitive and egocentric poet, and the sometimes terrible effect of that stereotype on a generation of poets. In different ways, it had some force in their minds, in the minds of those who perceived them, and even in their work. But here is a poet whose subject was the self, and whose work, on the level of personality, takes that self (in a way) for granted, without a moment of extraneous self-regard or anxious preening. I don't mean to insult the memories of the other poets, but to think about a poetic tradition. Much of what readers love in English-language poetry began in the elaborate seduction poetry of the sixteenth century, in which the poet displayed the eloquence that might both win his beloved and preserve her (or him) for the ages, defying time. This sonneteer's self-admiration continues, possibly, even into such charming modern poems of personality as the one in which William Carlos Williams dances before the mirror naked while his family sleeps, twirling a shirt over his head: "who shall say," he asks, "that I am not the happy genius of my household?" It seems at least worth musing about whether Elizabeth Bishop's distinctive voice and material come partly from her ability to walk into the territory of the self and its ways with no least nuance of the peacock's strut.

Some readers will feel that Bishop's publishers should not have included the occasional poems, or the poems composed at the age of sixteen, though very few readers will resist reading them. (There is a spark in every one of them.) The volume also contains at least one extremely good previously "lost" poem, "Pleasure Seas." The jacket design uses a watercolor drawn by Elizabeth Bishop in Mexico in 1942. It is a light-hearted view of houses and windmills from a balcony, including the twin spires of a church, a water tower, palm trees, and what appear to be telephone poles. The perspective is from an angle of about forty-five degrees to the balcony railing in the foreground, and close to it, as if the artist and her pad were nearly there in the picture itself.

George Oppen: "The Undertaking"

One night a few years ago, not long before George Oppen died, he was honored by the San Francisco Bay Area PEN Society, along with other senior writers including Janet Lewis. There were several speeches, and some of these, I am sorry to say, emphasized the themes of neglect and resentment and regional venom. Being a writer was depicted as a thankless, bitter work. A Bay Area writer, the more thankless and bitter. Harsh things were said about Los Angeles, and about New York in general and *The New York Times Book Review* in particular. An unattractive, whining and snapping aspect of literary San Francisco—its defensiveness and self-righteousness and hunger for publicity—thrashed its tail and threatened to take over the occasion.

Janet Lewis, whose books of poetry and fiction remain in print, decade after decade, maintaining their loyal following and winning new initiates regardless of what the wheel of fashion lifts and drops and grinds away, listened with a patient, sunny demeanor. Josephine Miles spoke briefly, praising Lewis's ear for verbal music. All three of these senior artists seemed to have outgrown the provincialities of time and place. Physical grace seemed the outward sign of this inner balance. The intelligent peregrine tilt of Miles's head perched on her disabled body, Lewis's straight back and radiance, Oppen's incredible great oblong skull, each seemed to mime in its way the habit of unbound attention to the world.

Then the poet Jack Marshall brought a tape recorder to the front of the room, and we all listened to the voice of Oppen reading from "Of Being Numerous":

The great stone
Above the river
In the pylon of the bridge

'1875'

68

Frozen in the moonlight
In the frozen air over the footpath, consciousness

Which has nothing to gain, which awaits nothing,
Which loves itself

("Of Being Numerous," 5)

The luminous, simple detail of the specified year on the great bridge, above the river and over the traffic, is an emblem of an unbiased, free and convinced consciousness. This consciousness specifies, but what it specifies is historical and public, and its action is general, all but impersonal. And the implied action of Oppen's language, too, is toward the general, implying that even the city is not a place but a condition of mind, linked experiences over time:

The emotions are engaged
Entering the city
As entering any city.

We are not coeval
With a locality
But we imagine others are,

We encounter them. Actually
A populace flows
Thru the city.

("Of Being Numerous," 3)

That is, our immediate and particular encounter with the city would persuade us that it exists somewhere or somehow as a definite aggregate of people, buildings, artifacts. But the city is as much a flow in time as any one person's emotional experience of it:

For the people of that flow
Are new, the old

New to age as the young
To youth

("Of Being Numerous," 4)

And because that flow is a new, communal circumstance, "This is a language, therefore," he says, "of New York." The language will be communal and informed by history more than it is personal and informed by locale. Its compression will often be the compression of generality.

This is one way to describe the particular genius in Oppen's work, its contribution to our poetry: the way in which it tends ultimately toward the general. Contrast his lines on the year carved into the pylon of the bridge with Williams's numeral:

THE GREAT FIGURE

Among the rain
and lights
I saw the figure 5
in gold
on a red
firetruck
moving
tense
unheeded
to gong clangs
siren howls
and wheels rumbling
through the dark city.

The four digits "1875" framed in Oppen's quotation marks have a presence that is manifold because it is historical. The 5 on the firetruck is swathed in the mystery and violence of the particular city on this one wet night. The consciousness embodied on the pylon is public, "frozen," lofty; the passing 5 is "unheeded" unless heeded by the poet. It is the difference between the mystery of experience, evoked in Williams's poem, and the mystery of meaning, in Oppen's. I suppose that embedded in this distinction is the seed of the scope and force that make Williams the greater artist, even as it suggests Oppen's particular spirit.

Another way to describe that spirit is to say that it is the opposite of "regional." Born into a kind of petty nobility of San Francisco, in a well-off German Jewish family, the poet seems to have expressed his aristocratic, cosmopolitan background by choosing, very early in life, disinterested idealism and art. San Francisco, New York, Paris, Maine, Los Angeles, Mexico, were places in a lifetime, each with its color and none a sufficient microcosm. The xenophobic tribute of that night in San Francisco was profoundly inappropriate, because the flux of human life through a place, for such a sensibility, is always more crucial than the peculiarities of the place. A poem from *The Materials* will illustrate what I mean:

THE UNDERTAKING IN NEW JERSEY

Beyond the Hudson's
Unimportant water lapping
In the dark against the city's shores
Are the small towns, remnants
Of forge and coal yard. The bird's voice in their streets
May not mean much: a bird the age of a child chirping
At curbs and curb gratings,
At barber shops and townsmen
Born of girls—
Of girls! Girls gave birth . . . But the interiors
Are the women's: curtained,
Lit, the fabric
To which the men return. Surely they imagine
Some task beyond the window glass
And the fabrics as if an eventual brother
In the fields were nourished by all this in country
Torn by the trucks where towns
And the flat boards of homes
Visibly move at sunrise and the trees
Carry quickly into daylight the excited birds.

The heavy trucks and the rising sun, both, make these dwellings visibly move, and carry the roused birds into the air. This inclusion of the human, commercial fabric along with the natural fabric reflects the hopeful humanity that imagines a nourishing link between what people do to make a life, domestically, and what people do in the unpromising commercial landscape of the river, the fields and the roads. The poet's imagination—the tentative optimism of "surely"—accords with the imagination that lights and curtains the house. The brother is "eventual" not just temporally but in the old, logician's sense of contingent: dependent upon the barely seen, vital civilization of the homes. On that civilization, not a collection of particular artifacts or fetishes or holy grounds, but rather a process or undertaking, everything depends.

And the "color" of these towns on the Jersey side of the Hudson is, like the water, unimportant. It is the idea he finds in the scene that matters. The generic term "bird" is important to the emotion: "sparrow" or "nuthatch" would distract feeling into the world of the naturalist, away from the great general undertaking. The place is to begin with particular, in the historical context embodied by place names, but then it is made as starkly representative as the "1875" frozen in moonlight. Where the regional spirit would linger, this other force—what should it be called?—surges up and away, with its wider, colder and more aspiring vision.

Oppen says that his poem is "a language of New York"—not *"the* language of New York." In keeping with the movement toward generality, his idiom achieves purity, a plain, fluent manner that is neither from the street on one side nor books on the other. He is not one of the writers who finds the eloquence or jazzy brilliance in American speech. On the other hand, his idiom doesn't retreat all the way into literature, away from the quiet precisions that distinguish nimbly (for example) between being brought down by someone or put down by them, putting up with someone or putting them up. His idiom has the purity of the old idea of a middle style, limber and penetrating rather than grand or flashing:

BOY'S ROOM

A friend saw the rooms
Of Keats and Shelley
At the lake, and saw 'they were just
Boys' rooms' and was moved

By that. And indeed a poet's room
Is a boy's room
And I suppose that women know it.

Perhaps the unbeautiful banker
Is exciting to a woman, a man

Not a boy gasping
For breath over a girl's body.

Mild comedy, meditation and balance here conspire almost as if
there were an American Ben Jonson, quietly deflecting expectation
with the vague "At the lake" and a direct quotation not from the
immortals but from a scrap of speech, unremarkable in itself. As the
high and the particular are put mildly in their places—which are
not here, but elsewhere—the poetic imagination is also put in its
place, by such calm, understated touches as the difference between
"woman" and "girl." (And between "beautiful" and "exciting.")
The style of speech finds the hidden distinction in the plain "just
boys' rooms" and accommodates it with that degree of formality
represented by "indeed" and "perhaps."

I have associated this style of speech and perception with a spirit
that is the opposite of regional, and it is hard to find the right name
for that opposite. "Cosmopolitan" and "urbane" have all the wrong
social connotations, and I think all the other derivatives of *urbs* and
polis suggest too much the site for cocktails or parades. I want to
call it "town" or "marketplace," the culture and manners of making
a living and conversation, but not of marching or the museum:

Phyllis—not neo-classic,
The girl's name is Phyllis—

Coming home from her first job
On the bus in the bare civic interior
Among those people, the small doors
Opening on the night, at the curb
Her heart, she told me, suddenly tight with happiness—

So small a picture,
A spot of light on the curb, it cannot demean us

I too am in love down there with the streets
And the square slabs of pavement—

To talk of the house and the neighborhood and the docks

And it is not 'art'

                                        ("Of Being Numerous," 11)

Perhaps the idea of a street, the linear conduit and marketplace, is the best analogue in locale for this idiom and frame of mind, the civic interior of the bus with its aperture onto the curb, the house and neighborhood and docks. Not the gasping at beauty of the Romantic poet, and not heroic or " 'art'," the street and bus are not Whitmanian because they are not made heroic by the poet's embrace. They remain what they were: part of "the undertaking," functional and objective.

The road or street as a means toward somewhere and as a meeting place represents an ideal that is particular and personal, yet objective and of human culture at large—a way, rather than some one located monument or state. The striving together of individual people defines this general culture that accords with Oppen's style, a culture that often seems implicitly opposed to the idea of the hero or the idea of the masses:

I cannot even now
Altogether disengage myself
From those men

With whom I stood in emplacements, in mess tents,
In hospitals and sheds and hid in the gullies
Of blasted roads in a ruined country,

Among them many men
More capable than I—

Muykuyt and a sergeant
Named Healy,
That lieutenant also—

How forget that? How talk
Distantly of 'The People'

Who are that force
Within the walls
Of cities

Wherein their cars
Echo like history
Down walled avenues

In which one cannot speak.
　("Of Being Numerous," 14)

The initial idea here is familiar from many accounts of modern war.
Oppen's contribution to it is the peculiar blend of objectivity and
personal feeling, generality and specification: bringing walled cities
together with the hemming walls of modern city blocks, and the
homely American twentieth-century word "car" into a three-word
line with "Wherein" and the echoing of history.

The phrase "like history" becomes stranger and richer the more
one considers it. The effect is partly to imply inverted commas
around "history" like the ones around "art" in the passage of Phyllis
and the bus. The force or process of culture, the undertaking, which
is an ongoing process of change, is the force of all the particular
people in the street, yet somehow to be considered objectively, not
from some particular perspective. This contradiction-resolving ideal
is expressed through the figure of a roadway in the eighth section
of the poem "Route":

Cars on the highway filled with speech,
People talk, they talk to each other;

Imagine a man in the ditch,
The wheels of the overturned wreck
Still spinning—

I don't mean he despairs, I mean if he does not
He sees in the manner of poetry

What we say to one another in our "civic interiors" as they move
along is not poetry, but poetry sees in a manner that is linked to
that speech, yet objective, not quite part of the hurrying traffic.
Conversely, poetry sees the wreck (as this poem ends with vision
of cataclysm), yet remains loyal to the daily particular traffic, the

actual individual speech of the cars in the streets and of the houses along the streets and rivers.

That paradoxical ideal, and Oppen's many realizations of it, are inspiring. There are limitations to the ideal, and there are sometimes defects in the realizations, parts of his work that are awkward or flat or too derivative of Pound or Williams. His true terrain is one that belongs to neither Pound nor Williams, and it seems to have a vital importance of its own, as well as an immense sweetness. In "Of Being Numerous" he describes himself as one of those who have made poetry "from nothing but man's way of thought and one of his dialects and what has happened to me."

The uninflated confidence and modesty of that sentence, its freedom from the biases of perspective, are suitably embodied by the image of the poet listening to his own voice reading from the tape recorder: full of an impersonal and unembarrassed attention—one of an audience, his head gently tilted to hear, listening to his own voice and words with the bearing of the most alert among us, the least self-conscious.

Seamus Heaney's Island

This splendid book of poems by the author of *North* and *Field Work* is divided into three parts: an opening section of lyric poems including some as good as his best; a central sequence inspired by Dante; and a concluding section in which the mythological Irish king Sweeney appears to observe contemporary Ireland, its literary life in particular, with an irritable, untamed eye.

The texture of the language, chunky and clabbered, full of strong joined stresses and clipped precision, resembles that of Heaney's earlier books. It is a medium that has won readers over because it is both dense and clear. Here is the conclusion of *"Iron Spike"*:

And the sledge-head that sank it
with a last opaque report
deep into the creosoted
sleeper, where is that?

And the sweat-cured haft?
Ask the ones in the buggy,
inaudible and upright
and sped along without shadows.

Significantly, these lines have to do with the partial, ghostly, nevertheless definite survival of the past into the present, and the double action of pulling the solid past out of the earth while also questioning its vaporous, "inaudible" ghost. This is a great central area of the book, and perhaps of Heaney's career: the past, and what lost in the past must be retrieved, or what surviving from it cannot be evaded or comprehended.

Another poem from *Station Island*'s first section, "Changes," begins with two people taking a walk; for one of them it is a walk

A review of *Station Island* (Farrar, Straus & Giroux, 1985) by Seamus Heaney.

into the past (almost in the spirit of Thomas Hardy, invoked in another of these poems):

> As you came with me in silence
> to the pump in the long grass
>
> I heard much that you could not hear:
> the bite of the spade that sank it,
>
> the slithering and grumble
> as the mason mixed his mortar,
>
> and women coming with white buckets
> like flashes on their ruffled wings.

When he opens the iron lid of the pump, he and the child discover a bird nesting there. Then he shuts it and gently opens it again, to disclose at first only a single egg, with the bird hidden "in the rusted bend of the spout" where "tail feathers splayed and sat tight." "Sat tight" in just two syllables clinches a rhyme, wittily transforms a cliché, and finds an image for the present moment, balanced between remote past and distant future.

The ending of the poem raises interesting questions of comparison between Heaney and his American contemporaries. After the image of the bird, the poet addresses the child:

> So tender, I said, "Remember this.
> It will be good for you to retrace this path
>
> when you have grown away and stand at last
> at the very centre of the empty city."

Honoring this poem, I also wonder tentatively if an American poet could oppose the rustic past and the urban future quite so completely and tenderly, in so direct a line with Yeats's opposition of Innisfree and the "pavement gray."

That is, on the one hand Heaney's work resembles some of the recent American books that have made strong impressions on me, resembles them both in subject matter and in an approach to technique that seems "post-modernist." For Heaney as for these American contemporaries formal freedom feels assumed, and matters of technique no longer fighting issues in the old modernist sense. The personal past, in Frank Bidart's *The Sacrifice* or Louise Gluck's *Descending Figure,* and the national past in C. K. Williams's *Tar* or Alfred Corn's *Notes from a Child of Paradise,* correspond to elements in Heaney's material.

But on the other hand, there was no Irish or English William Carlos Williams to challenge the idea of "the empty city" with this particular note:

Chimneys, roofs, fences of
wood and metal in an unfenced

age and enclosing next to
nothing at all: the old man
in a sweater and soft black
hat who sweeps the sidewalk—

his own ten feet of it—
in a wind that fitfully
turning his corner has
overwhelmed the entire city

This kind of vital "next to nothing at all," in these cadences, has been grafted deeply into American poets' idea of their art. It seems to me that Heaney may have a different sense of urban life from that of his American colleagues, and with it a different sense of poetic form, so that the gentleness and grace of his cadences and language, in a poem like this one, tell us a somewhat different story from our own. And that is another reason to value and re-read poems like "Changes."

With characteristic wit and penetration, Heaney has given the book, and its central sequence, a title of many senses. A station is a place where one must stand, or habitually stands, and because "station" is a military, social and religious term—denoting steps in a pilgrimage as well as the stations of the cross—the idea of a station recalls the whole web of inherited communal ties and responsibilities. In seeming opposition, "island" suggests isolation; but the terms reverse in relation to Heaney's country, Ireland, which is an island, and an island whose artists have sometimes stationed themselves somewhat apart from those inherited ties.

It is also characteristic of Heaney's shrewd attention to the world around him that he took the term from experience, personal and communal. Station Island is an island on Lough Derg, in County Donegal, also called St. Patrick's Purgatory, where pilgrims still go for a three-day exercise that includes "stations" re-creating Patrick's vigil and fasting on the site. The poem is bold enough to be consciously Dantesque in elements like its encounters with figures from the poet's life, and tactful and wise enough that the project does not seem overweening or vainglorious.

One striking thing about the sequence is how strong the narrative is: so artful and so at home with the verse that the best sections deserve comparison with Frost's narrative poems. Even more than the previous books, this one establishes that along with his wonderful gifts of eye and ear, Heaney has the gift of the storyteller. The power to tell a story compactly, in a way that suggests that it could be told with such force only in verse, appears with particular clarity in the poem's seventh section, where the poet encounters the victim of a political killing, an admired schoolmate and football teammate ("the one stylist on the team"):

> And though I was reluctant
> I turned to meet his face and the shock
>
> is still in me at what I saw. His brow
> was blown open above the eye and blood
> had dried on his neck and cheek. "Easy now,"
>
> he said, "it's only me. You've seen men as raw
> after a football match . . . What time it was
> when I was wakened up I still don't know
>
> but I heard this knocking, knocking, and it
> scared me, like the phone in the small hours,
> so I had the sense not to put on the light
>
> but looked out from behind the curtain."

I find it hard to stop quoting; this section is a poem you might want to read aloud to friends, and the more of it you hear or read, the more impressive it is. But there is enough to admire in the quoted fragment: the way the full and partial rhymes shape the march of syntax without hobbling it, echoing the great model's *terza rima* just enough; the way the language is colloquial without windiness or strain; the rapid, natural transitions from the poet's voice to the interlocutor's, and from description to narrative; small telling contrasts between heightening ("knocking, knocking") and lowering ("I had the sense"), so that the elements of the divine and of human comedy become credible.

Just the same, at some point Heaney decided not to write an epic, decided that this work was not going to be as large as that. The sections and their actions stand out in stronger relief than the action of the whole, which is the poet's gathering of himself for new pastures. He chooses to pay homage to the past, rather than to re-create it as an epitome or global whole. This measured loyalty, a kind of quit-fee to the past, is the sequence's theme and its limiting boundary.

In the first section, he meets a kind of village bad-man who cuts wood on Sunday, "with a bow-saw, held / stiffly up like a lyre"; "Stay clear of all processions," this figure advises. In subsequent poems, the interlocutors are various of the empowered dead: historical figures, like the nineteenth-century Protestant convert and author William Carleton, or James Joyce, who has the last word.

Before that last word, the poet pays debts and respects, some of them to fosterers and alter-selves: to a parish priest who died young on a mission to Africa, a teacher, a childhood sweetheart, a fanatic young political thug dead in prison, a murdered cousin the poet has written about, who questions whether that writing—an earlier, memorable poem in *Field Work*—was true enough:

"The Protestant who shot me through the head
I accuse directly, but indirectly, you
who now atone perhaps upon this bed
for the way you whitewashed ugliness and drew
the lovely blinds of the *Purgatorio*
and saccharined my death with morning dew."

This atonement is more like a discharged responsibility than a life's project: an island of devotion rather than an extended path of pilgrimage. ("Bed" here means one of the stone circles, perhaps once monastic cells, on Station Island, at which one prays.) The last of such payments, in the penultimate poem, is given to a fondly remembered priest who once said, "Read poems as prayers . . . and for your penance / translate me something by Juan de la Cruz." The translation is elegantly grave and straightforward, and precedes the final encounter with Joyce.

As if echoing the profane woodcutter of the first section, the severe word-crafter, with his voice "eddying with the vowels of all rivers," counsels against all processions in his own way. He greets the poet on the tarmac of the parking lot, not on the island itself, and urges work-lust, independence, freedom from the dead fires of the past, and uncumbered adventure into "the dark of the whole sea." In the poem's last line, isolated and single after the processional of tercets, "the downpour loosed its screens round his straight walk."

Those concluding two words, with their implication of a strict course, exactingly defined (though into a shrouded and stormswept terrain), indicate in a way that the sequence is less a summing-up than a tentative pointing forward. The sequence successfully evokes its great predecessors partly by declining their epic terms. In any case, the book as a whole is a rich and commanding work, one more indication that Seamus Heaney is a leading figure in a generation of poets that may be making already, and partly unnoticed, a new, various and powerful poetry in English.

Responsibilities of the Poet

Certain general ideas come up repeatedly, in various guises, when contemporary poetry is discussed. One of these might be described as the question of what, if anything, is our social responsibility as poets.

That is, there are things a poet may owe the art of poetry—work, perhaps. And in a sense there are things writers owe themselves—emotional truthfulness: attention toward one's own feelings. But what, if anything, can a poet be said to owe other people in general, considered as a community? For what is the poet answerable? This is a more immediate—though more limited—way of putting the question than such familiar terms as "political poetry."

Another recurring topic is what might be called Poetry Gloom. I mean the sourness and kvetching that sometimes come into our feelings about our art: the mysterious disaffections, the querulous doubts, the dispirited mood in which we ask ourselves, has contemporary poetry gone downhill, does anyone at all read it, has poetry become a mere hobby, do only one's friends do it well, and so forth. This matter often comes up in the form of questions about the "popularity" or "audience" of poetry.

Possibly the appetite for poetry really was greater in the good old days, in other societies. After the total disaster at Syracuse, when the Athenians, their great imperialist adventure failed, were being massacred, or branded as slaves with the image of a horse burned into the forehead, a few were saved for the sake of Euripides, whose work, it seems, was well thought of by the Syracusans. "Many of the captives who got safe back to Athens," writes Plutarch,

> are said, after they reached home, to have gone and made their acknowledgments to Euripides, relating how some of them had

A "craft lecture" to the Napa Poetry Conference, August 1984.

been released from their slavery by teaching what they could re-
member of his poems and others, when straggling after the fight,
had been relieved with meat and drink for repeating some of his
lyrics.

This is enviable; but I think that at some vital level our answer must
be, *so what?* Jarrell wrote about those people who say they "just
can't read modern poetry" in a tone that implies their happiest hours
are spent in front of the fireplace with a volume of Blake or Racine.
To court such readers, or to envy Euripides, would be understand-
able, but futile, impulses.

And I think they are even frivolous impulses, beside the point.
Of course every artist is in competition with the movies, in the sense
that art tries to be as interesting as it can. But tailoring one's work
to an audience any less hungry for one's art than oneself probably
makes for bad movies and bad poems. And whether that is true or
not, most poets would be bad at such tailoring anyway. Daydreams
aside, more urgent questions are: what is our job? And: what are the
roots of good and bad morale about it?

The second question is strange, if I am right in supposing that
poetry is the very art of being interesting. The two most interesting
things in the world, for our species, are ideas and the individual
human body, two elements that poetry uniquely joins together. It
is the nature of poetry to emphasize constantly that the physical
sounds of words come from a particular body, one at a time, in a
certain order. By memorizing lines of Euripides, the Athenian
soldiers had incorporated certain precise shades of conception. This
dual concern, bodily and conceptual, is what Pound means by saying
that poetry is a centaur: prose hits the target with its arrow; poetry
does the same from horseback. If you are too stupid, or too cerebral,
you may miss half of it.

Here I arrive at the relation between the two questions, morale
and responsibility. In the root sense of the glamourless word "re-
sponsibility," people crave not only answers but also answerability.
Involving a promise or engagement, the word is related to "spon-
sor" and "spouse." We want our answers to be craved as in the
testing and reassuring of any animal parent and child, or the mutual
nudge and call of two liturgical voices. The corporeal, memorizable
quality of verse carries with it a sense of social exchange. The visible

image of the horse burned into the living human body says one thing; the memorized cadence of words, without exactly contradicting that statement, answers it with another.

An artist needs not so much an audience, as to feel a need to answer, a promise to respond. The response may be a contradiction, it may be unwanted, it may go unheeded, it may be embraced but twisted (William Blake the most quoted author in the modern House of Commons!)—but it is owed, and the sense that it is owed is a basic requirement for the poet's good feeling about the art. This need to answer, as firm as a borrowed object or a cash debt, is the ground where the centaur walks.

A critic, a passionate writer on poetry, culture and politics, once said to me, "When I ask American poets if they are concerned about United States foreign policy in Latin America, they all say yes, they are. But practically none of them write about it: why not?"

My response to this question was not dazzling. "I don't know," I said. And then, thinking about it for another moment: "It certainly isn't that they don't want to." The desire to make a good work, or the desire to deal with a given subject—in theory, the desire to deal with every subject—isn't automatically fulfilled.

The desire to see, and the desire to feel obliged to answer, are valuable, perhaps indispensable parts of the poet's feelings about the art. But in themselves they are not enough. In some way, before an artist can see a subject—foreign policy, or any other subject—the artist must transform it: answer the received cultural imagination of the subject with something utterly different. This need to answer by transforming is primary; it comes before everything else.

Something of the kind may explain the interesting phenomenon of bad work by good artists. Even a gifted, hard-working writer with a large and appreciative audience may write badly, I think, if this sense of an obligation to answer—a promised pushing-back or responding—is lacking. Irresponsibility subtly deadens the work. Conversely, a dutiful editorializing work, devoid of the kind of transformation I mean, may also be dead.

To put it differently, the idea of social responsibility seems to raise a powerful contradiction, in the light of another intuited principle, freedom. The poet needs to feel utterly free, yet answerable. This paradox underlies and confounds much discussion of our art; poetry is so bodily and yet so explicit, so capable of subjects and yet so subtly transforming of them, that it seems recurrently to be quite like the rest of life, and yet different.

One anecdotal example: I have a friend who drives a car impatiently, sometimes with a vivid running commentary on other drivers. One day while I sat next to him the car in front of us behaved in a notably indecisive, unpredictable, petulant, dog-in-the-manger manner. But my friend was calm, he did not gesture and he certainly did not honk. I asked him why, and his explanation was, "I never hassle anybody who is taking care of small children."

This self-conscious respect for child care seems to me more than simply sweet. It exemplifies a basic form of social responsibility, an element of communal life more basic even than the boss-and-henchmen *comitatus* celebrated in *Beowulf*. People in a bus or restaurant where there is a small child like to think, I believe, that in an emergency they would protect the child, despite gulfs of social class or race or mere difference that might intervene.

The feeling is not goodness, exactly, but rather the desire to think well of ourselves—the first civic virtue, the fission of subject and object emitting the bubble reputation. That desire is part of our nature as social animals whose hairless, pudgy offspring pass through a long period of learning and vulnerability. We live together, rather than separately like Cyclopes, or otherwise perish in a generation. We living in our majority need to mediate between the dead, who took care of us, and not only the young, but the unborn.

And as poets, too, one of our responsibilities is to mediate between the dead and the unborn: we must feel ready to answer, as if asked by the dead if we have handed on what they gave us, or asked by the unborn what we have for them. This is one answer, the great conservative answer, to the question of what responsibility the poet bears to society. By practicing an art learned partly from the dead, one keeps it alive for the unborn.

Arts do, after all, die. In a way it is their survival that is surprising. When I was in primary school, they showed us films provided by the paper industry or the glass industry depicting, with diagrams and footage of incredibly elaborate machines, the steps in making the innumerable kinds of paper, or glass jars and lenses and fiberglass curtains and fuselages. I remember thinking with some panic that it would soon all decay and fall apart: that the kids I knew in my own generation would be unable to learn those complex processes in time. When the adults died, we would botch the machines; I knew this with certainty, because I knew my peers and myself.

This fear still makes sense to me, and yet some of us went on not only to master those arcane processes and elaborate machines, but to improve them. Some people who were grubby, bored ten-year-olds in 1950 are now experts in fiber-optic controls in the manufacturing of semi-vitreous components, or in the editing of Provençal manuscripts.

So one great task we have to answer for is the keeping of an art that we did not invent, but were given, so that others who come after us can have it if they want it, as free to choose it and change it as we have been. A second task has been defined by Carolyn Forché, in a remarkable essay,[1] as "a poetry of witness": we must use the art to behold the actual evidence before us. We must answer for what we see.

Witness may or may not involve advocacy, and the line between the two will be drawn differently by each of us; but the strange truth about witness is that though it may include both advocacy and judgment, it includes more than them, as well. If political or moral advocacy were all we had to answer for, that would be almost easy. Witness goes further, I think, because it involves the challenge of not flinching from the evidence. It proceeds from judgment to testimony.

In the most uncompromising sense, this means that whatever important experience seems least poetic to me is likely to be my job. Forché, for example, writes:

> In those days I kept my work as a poet and journalist separate, of two distinct *mentalités,* but I could not keep El Salvador from my poems because it had become so much a part of my life. I was cautioned to avoid mixing art and politics, that one damages the other, and it was some time before I realized that "political poetry" often means the poetry of protest, accused of polemical didacticism, and not the poetry which implicitly celebrates politically acceptable values.[2]

[1]Carolyn Forché, "El Salvador: An Aide Memoire," *American Poetry Review,* July/August 1981, vol. 10, no. 4, pp. 3–7.
[2]*Ibid.,* p. 6.

That is, the poet realized that what had seemed "unpoetic" or fit only for journalism, because it was supposedly contaminated with particular political implications, was her task. The "contamination" or "politics" was her responsibility, what she had to answer for as if she had promised something about it when she undertook the art of poetry. A corollary realization is that "all poetry is political": what is politically acceptable to some particular observer may seem "unpolitical" to that observer.

Where does the debilitating falseness come from, that tempts us to look away from evidence, or fit it into some allegedly "poetic" pattern, with the inevitable result of Poetry Gloom? Forché continues, a few sentences later:

> From our tradition we inherit a poetic, a sense of appropriate subjects, styles, forms and levels of diction; that poetic might insist that we be attuned to the individual in isolation, to particular sensitivity in the face of "nature," to special ingenuity in inventing metaphor.[3]

The need to notice, to include the evidence as a true and reliable witness, can be confused and blunted by the other, conserving responsibility of mediation between the dead and the unborn. And just as society can vaguely, quietly diffuse an invisible, apparently "apolitical" political ideology, culture can efficiently assimilate and enforce an invisible idea of what is poetic. In a dim view of the dialectic, it seems that society's tribute to poetry is to incorporate each new, at first resisted sense of the poetic, and so to spread it— and blunt it—for each new generation. Even while seeming not to taste each new poetic, the world swallows it.

Two nearly paradoxical formulations emerge from this conflict. First, only the challenge of what may seem unpoetic, that which has not already been made poetic by the tradition, can keep the art truly pure and alive. Put to no new use, the art rots. Second, the habits and visions of the art itself, which we are responsible for keeping alive, can seem to conspire against that act of use or witness. The material or rhetoric that seems already, on the face of it, proper to

[3]*Ibid.*

poetry may have been made poetic already by Baudelaire, or Wordsworth, or Rilke, or Neruda.

To put it simply, and only a little fancifully, we have in our care and for our use and pleasure a valuable gift, and we must answer both for preserving it, and for changing it. And the second we fail to make good answer on either score, the gift stops giving pleasure, and makes us feel bad, instead.

Since there is no way to say what evidence will seem pressing but difficult to a given artist—Central America, the human body, the nature of art, taking care of one's paraplegic sister, theology, farming, American electoral politics, the ideological meaning of free verse, the art of domestic design—no subject ever is forbidden. Society depends on the poet to witness something, and yet the poet can discover that thing only by looking away from what society has learned to see poetically.

Thus, there is a dialectic between the poet and culture: the culture presents us with poetry, and with implicit definitions of what materials and means are poetic. The answer we must promise to give is "no." Real works revise the received idea of what poetry is; by mysterious cultural means the revisions are assimilated and then presented as the next definition to be resisted, violated and renewed. What poets must answer for is the unpoetic. And before we can identify it, or witness it, an act of judgment is necessary. This act of judgment can only be exemplified.

Here is one of the most valued poems in our language. In quoting the poem, I particularly want to point out the insistently repeated absolutes, especially the words *"every"* and *"most"*:

LONDON

I wander thro' each charter'd street,
Near where the charter'd Thames does flow,
And mark in every face I meet
Marks of weakness, marks of woe.

In every cry of every Man,
In every Infant's cry of fear,
In every voice, in every ban,
The mind-forg'd manacles I hear:

How the Chimney-sweeper's cry
Every blackening Church appalls,
And the hapless Soldier's sigh
Runs in blood down Palace walls.

But most thro' midnight streets I hear
How the youthful Harlot's curse
Blasts the new-born Infant's tear
And blights with plagues the Marriage hearse.

The word "every" throbs through all of the stanzas except the final one, repeated five times in the drumlike second stanza. This insistent chain of "every's" leads to the capping, climactic movement of the conclusion, with its contrary, superlative *"But most"*: the immense force of the ending comes partly from the way "But most" piles its weight onto the already doubled and redoubled momentum of "every" and "every" and "every."

One thing that "every" and "every" brings into the poem is the sense of a social whole: it is all of us, we are part of it, no utter exception is possible, it is like a family, and a family that bears a "mark." And though my brother and not I may have poured your blood or blighted your tear, it would be stupid of me to think that your response to me—or mine to you—could go uncolored by what you know of my family. The poem witnesses the legal entity of a city in a way that transforms it into this social whole.

Blake's "most" is reserved for the blighting of future generations —the extension of social corruption forward, into the future, through the infection of those still *in utero*. This continuation forward in time of the omnipresent blight and pain, under the climactic "but most," suggests both of the broad kinds of answerability: it is literally conservative, and it reminds us that we are witnesses for the future. Those who want to know about London in Blake's time read this poem. They may read the contemporary journalism, as well, but for an inward understanding of such evidence, they will again read Blake. If someone in the future wants to understand *Newsweek* and *Time,* or the *CBS Evening News,* our poems must answer to the purpose. We are supposed to mark the evidence, as well as continuing the art.

In "London," all this is accomplished by the violently wholesale quality of what is "marked" in both senses, witnessed and scarred. The "unpoetic" part of the poem is the rhetoric that invents or enacts the vision of society as a kind of nightmarish, total family rather than an orderly contractual, chartered arrangement. In a sense, Blake had to transform the city imaginatively, put the mark of his judgment upon it, in order to portray it in the mock-hymn of "London."

If all poems were like "London," the question might seem relatively simple. But not all poems invite a social understanding of themselves nearly as strongly as this. And few of us were attracted to poetry to start with by the idea of being a good witness, still less the idea of mediating between the dead and the unborn. Most of us were attracted to poetry because of language that gave us enormous, unmistakable pleasure: not only the physical pleasure of beaded bubbles winking at the brim, but also the intellectual pleasure of thinking of the thin men of Haddam who rode over Connecticut in a glass coach, how they are both creatures of fantasy and suburban commuters on the train.

Such transformation seems to precede witness, in the working of poetry and in the history of our need for poetry. Its relation to witness is like that suggested by a passage in Ben Jonson's great poem "To Heaven":

As thou art all, so be thou all to me,
First, midst, and last, converted one, and three;
My faith, my hope, my love: and in this state
My judge, my witness, and my advocate.

Faith in the absolute fairness of a judge like the Father is parallel to hope regarding a witness (the Holy Ghost) and love for an advocate, whose Christian mercy extends beyond justice. In keeping with the biblical and religious models, the transforming certainty of judgment precedes the processes of witness and advocacy. Jonson's intellectually elegant revision of the courtroom sequence (evidence, argument, judgment) reflects the way that poetry seems to depend upon a prior and tremendously confident process of transformation.

Transformation, too, is a social role of poetry: its oldest, clearest form must be epideictic, the praising of heroes, celebrating one whose physical or moral gifts have brought gain or glory to the tribe: the woman in Robinson's "Eros Turannos," whose catastrophic love affair makes "all the town and harbor side / Vibrate with her seclusion" is a peculiar, American provincial version of such a figure. She makes the town more heroic, and the gossiping townfolk make her story more heroic:

> She fears him, and will always ask
>   What fated her to choose him;
> She meets in his engaging mask
>   All reasons to refuse him;
> But what she meets and what she fears
> Are less than are the downward years
> Drawn slowly to the foamless weirs
>   Of age, were she to lose him.
>
> Between a blurred sagacity
>   That once had power to sound him,
> And Love, that will not let him be
>   The Judas that she found him,
> Her pride assuages her almost,
> As if it were alone the cost.—
> He sees that he will not be lost,
>   And waits and looks around him.
>
> A sense of ocean and old trees
>   Envelops and allures him;
> Tradition, touching all he sees,
>   Beguiles and reassures him;
> And all her doubts of what he says
> Are dimmed with what she knows of days—
> Till even prejudice delays,
>   And fades, and she secures him.
>
> The falling leaf inaugurates
>   The reign of her confusion;
> The pounding wave reverberates
>   The dirge of her illusion;

And home, where passion lived and died,
Becomes a place where she can hide,
While all the town and harbor side
    Vibrate with her seclusion.

We tell you, tapping on our brows,
    The story as it should be,—
As if the story of a house
    Were told, or ever could be;
We'll have no kindly veil between
Her visions and those we have seen,—
As if we guessed what hers have been,
    Or what they are or would be.

Meanwhile we do no harm; for they
    That with a god have striven,
Not hearing much of what we say,
    Take what the god has given;
Though like waves breaking it may be,
Or like a changed familiar tree,
Or like a stairway to the sea
    Where down the blind are driven.

The mean-minded little town, the superior, desperate woman, the vulgar man, even perhaps the complacent, spavined literary culture whose editors had no use for Robinson's work, all are resisted and transformed by a rhetoric that includes the coming together of the poem's peculiar form, its powerful narrative, and the heroic symbol of the ocean.

Formally, the resistant or "unpoetic" element in "Eros Turannos" is a kind of hypertrophy. As if in response to an insufficiently communal or folkloric relation between artist and audience, or heroine and community—even between the seemingly omniscient narrator of the beginning and the "we" speaking the ending—the poem exaggerates the formal, communal elements of the poem. With its feminine rhymes and triple rhymes and extension of ballad structure the poem is almost a parody ballad. The hypertrophy of traditional folk or ritualistic formal means resists an idea of poetic language, and of poetry in relation to social reality, by exaggeration. In its own terms this virtuoso exaggeration is as violent as the sweeping terms of Blake's "London," with its angry formal remaking of the hymn.

Based on a mighty, prior act of transforming judgment, "London" takes the rhetorical mode of witnessing ("I mark"); what is on trial is a transformed London, and the poet's eye roams through it like the Holy Ghost, seeing more than any literal social reality could make possible. His repeated "every" is in part a mark of ubiquity. Robinson's poem of tragic celebration, full of mercy and advocacy in relation to its heroine, evokes images and rhetoric of judgment; and judgment is formally emphasized almost to the point of parody by the quality of incantation. Yet the perspective in "Eros Turannos," too, is preternatural. Certainly, the viewpoint is more than socially located. It is the multiple perspective of the ubiquitous witness:

> Meanwhile we do no harm; for they
>   That with a god have striven,
> Not hearing much of what we say,
>   Take what the god has given;
> Though like waves breaking it may be
> Or like a changed familiar tree,
> Or like a stairway to the sea
>   Where down the blind are driven.

What "we" see or say; what is known of "her" fears and questions; what "they" hear or take; what the god gives; what "it" may be like—all of these narrated materials gain their authority from the underlying, invisible certainty of transformation. That certainty appears in the "changed familiar tree," and its invisible, generative power leads to the stairway "Where down the blind are driven." The poet's own voice changes from impersonal omniscience at the outset to a communal first-person plural by the close.

These examples suggest to me that society forms an idea of the poetic, an idea which has its implications about social reality, and that the poet needs to respond by answering with a rebuttal or transformation of terms. But what about a poem that is deliberately irresponsible, that is anarchic or unacceptable in its social attitude? What, for example, about Frank O'Hara's poem "Ave Maria"?

Mothers of America
                    let your kids go to the movies!
get them out of the house so they won't know what you're up to
it's true fresh air is good for the body
                              but what about the soul
that grows in darkness, embossed by silvery images
and when you grow old as grow old you must
                                        they won't hate you
they won't criticize you they won't know
                              they'll be in some glamorous country
they first saw on a Saturday afternoon or playing hookey

they may even be grateful to you
                              for their first sexual experience
which only cost you a quarter
                              and didn't upset the peaceful home
they will know where candy bars come from
                              and gratuitous bags of popcorn
as gratuitous as leaving the movie before it's over
with a pleasant stranger whose apartment is in the
                              Heaven on Earth Bldg
near the Williamsburg Bridge
                    oh mothers you will have made the little tykes
so happy because if nobody does pick them up in the movies
they won't know the difference
                    and if somebody does it'll be sheer gravy
and they'll have been truly entertained either way
instead of hanging around the yard
                              or up in their room
                                        hating you
prematurely since you won't have done anything horribly mean
                                                  yet
except keeping them from the darker joys
                              it's unforgivable the latter
so don't blame me if you won't take this advice
                              and the family breaks up
and your children grow old and blind in front of a TV set
                                        seeing
movies you wouldn't let them see when they were young.

The language of this poem dodges and charges so brilliantly on its way, with energy that is so happily demotic, that a reader is likely to want to keep up, to want to show that one can keep up. Among other things, the poem expresses love for the flawed, for imperfection—especially American imperfection—and the dark. O'Hara sprints happily through this terrain, leaping between such oppositions as "silvery images" versus "the peaceful home," to find the genuinely friendly, intimate and democratic note of "sheer gravy" and "so don't blame me if you won't take this advice." It is a contest between glamour and decency, apparently settled by an appeal to American idiom. His understanding of such speech, and by implication of the movies, is so clear and vivid that we want to share it, to assure ourselves that we, too, understand the dark, stained charm of Heaven on Earth as it appears in an actual New York. The language streaks forward impatiently and we want to go along.

One thing we are invited to go along with is the idea that children young enough to need permission to go to the movies may benefit from sexual use by adult strangers; that they may be grateful for it. Considered as advocacy, this is unacceptable: criminal, and worse. It is as if O'Hara chose the most repulsive proposition he could think of, to embed in the middle of his poem.

Various matters of rhetoric may soften or deflect the issue of unacceptability: since the group "Mothers of America" will for the most part not hear, and surely not heed, this oration, it can be looked on as not literal advocacy but mock-advocacy. And more legalistically, the seduction is conjectural: they *"may"* even be grateful. So the advocacy is hemmed by irony and disclaimer, with the outrageous jokes of "only cost you a quarter" and "sheer gravy" signaling how very much in the realm of rhetoric we are—an exuberant homosexual *schpritzing*.

But just the same, there is an element of the unacceptable in the poem, a violation of social boundaries. And far from seeming a regrettable, separable blemish, this repugnant element seems essential. It is what makes us believe the "darker joys," asking in effect if pleasure in the poem has a component of inexpensive, vicarious sexual naughtiness. Ultimately, I think it asks us to entertain the possibility of some one unusual eleven-year-old (should we imagine the lines as actual or fantasized autobiography?) who might conceivably feel grateful to his mother for the opportunity described.

In other words, the poem breaks or bends ideas about poetic method and content. And this resistant act seems prior to the poem, part of a preceding judgment that underlies what is seen and argued. Perhaps one thing I like in the poem is the daring with which it plays—and so clearly plays—at the definitive terms of judgment:

> keeping them from the darker joys
> it's unforgivable the latter

or the ratiocinative terms of advocacy:

> because if nobody does pick them up in the movies
> they won't know the difference
> and if somebody does it'll be sheer gravy

The democratic, almost conspirational note of "sheer gravy," and "horribly mean," deftly contrasted with language like "prematurely" and "the latter," invites an alliance in imperfection. The poem happily witnesses a great communal imperfection ("what you're up to," "horribly mean") and excitement in American life, all the grotesque, glorious fantasy life associated with the movies. The bite of the poem comes from its comic perspectives: the imagination of a scene where the poet addresses the Mothers, the imagination of the future at the end of the poem, the imagination of an idyllic sexual initiation for "tykes."

He is willing to share his sense of the movies, and of our culture, with us, and his willingness is rooted in his will to transform our idea of what is acceptable, in poetry or in the imagined oration itself. Other works of those late Eisenhower years get higher marks in the category "does not advocate awful crimes," but we do not read them with the pleasure and recognition this one gives, with its stern standard of being "truly entertained." In one way, the poem is a daring, ebullient prank; in another, it embodies the way a poet's vision and language spring from a need to resist and challenge what the culture has given.

"All poetry is political." The act of judgment prior to the vision of any poem is a social judgment. It always embodies, I believe, a resistance or transformation of communal values: Blake's indictment of totally visible, monolithic London; Robinson's dry rage that an aristocracy of grace and moral insight has no worldly force; O'Hara's celebration of what is cheerfully lawless in American life. Even when Emily Dickinson defines the ultimate privacy of the soul, she does it in terms that originate in social judgment:

> The soul selects her own Society—
> Then—shuts the Door.

As one of the best-known lines in contemporary poetry indicates, the unpredictable effect upon a community of what one writes may be less to the point than discharging the responsibility:

> America I'm putting my queer shoulder to the wheel.

The poet's first social responsibility, to continue the art, can be filled only through the second, opposed responsibility to change the terms of the art as given—and it is given socially, which is to say politically. What that will mean in the next poem anyone writes is by definition unknowable, with all the possibility of art.

II

AMERICAN POETRY AND
AMERICAN LIFE

I. Freneau, Whitman, Williams

I

We still face the classic question or challenge of American poetry, posed most sharply by Walt Whitman, and among the modernists by William Carlos Williams. What is, or what would be, a democratic poetry? What is the relation of an art reborn in European courts to vernacular culture?—or of American life to terms like "vernacular," which comes from *verna,* native or indigenous, denoting in Rome a slave born in his master's household?

I think that to say we are tired of the question, or to suppose we have resolved it, would be profoundly mistaken. From another angle, to say that the question, and poetry itself, are just not very important any more seems equally wrong. The question becomes ever more complicated and significant with our still expanding cultural imperium: our brilliant, immensely successful popular culture, the worldwide dominance of our music, clothes, movies, television, our gadgets, our gums and syrups. This fantastic power, a power partly of images, an overwhelming mixture of genius and sleaze, seems in different ways to make American poetry, and its relation to American life, both more important, and less.

I want to try approaching this area, vital but crusted over with cliché and confusion, through the beginnings of our country and its poetry in the eighteenth century. Back in the controversies and journalistic wars of the 1790s are some of the roots of living antagonisms and passions. Ezra Pound, in the "John Adams" cantos, is not the only modern American poet to hark back to the time of the country's founding. William Carlos Williams has written of Alexander Hamilton:

> Protector of liberty.
> Whose, Hamilton's?—to harness the whole, young aspiring genius to a treadmill? Paterson he wished to make capital of the country

because there was waterpower there which to his mind and time seemed colossal. And so he organized a company to hold the land thereabouts, with dams and sluices, the origin today of the vilest swillhole in christendom, the Passaic River; impossible to remove the nuisance so tight had he, Hamilton, sewed up his privileges unto kingdomcome, through his holding company, in the State legislature. *His* company. *His* United States: Hamiltonia—the land of the company.

Williams's attitude toward this "whole, young, aspiring genius" of the early United States is mixed. In the same section of *In the American Grain* he says:

> We are deceived by history. America had a great spirit given to freedom but it was a mean, narrow, provincial place; it was NOT the great liberty-loving country, not at all. Its choice spirits died.

Williams is the modern poet who has taken most seriously the Whitmanian charge to bring together poetry and democracy: which is to bring together the heritage of royal courts and the reality of American manners, a love of Keats's language and a sense of Keats's social circumstances. In these passages, Williams shows a sympathetic and familiar doubleness. It is not only that he is disgusted by the country's actual provinciality, meanness and narrowness on the one hand while celebrating its "aspiring genius" and "great spirit" on the other. Under that dual feeling is an irritable, restlessly energetic passion to sort out the provinciality, rawness and vulgarity that are the opposite of poetry from the defiant provinciality, the vital rawness and the saving vulgarity that are the sources of an American art. The ambivalence is buried in the trope of the Passaic River, the local flow of power that in its time was beautiful, untapped, colossal in its frame: the note of provincial nostalgia for that time when it "seemed colossal" is in subtle conflict with the hyperbolic disgust that denounces the vile—and dwindled—swillhole.

That double view—the poet celebrating the idea of democracy and liberty, the poet angry and despairing at the place, in the actual United States, of democracy, liberty and poetry—has been historically a kind of basic motive force. What is a poetry of liberty, and to paraphrase Williams's question about Hamilton, whose liberty, to do what? The mind floods, and sickens a little, with a list of actual literary responses, none without appeal, none truly adequate—referentially, to stir into poems a certain amount of baseball or Bo Diddley or Howdy Doody, or formally, to avoid sestinas and anapests, or critically, to yield the ground altogether to song lyrics or commercials, or ideologically, to avoid reference altogether. Trying to think past such a catalogue, I find that Williams's passionate resistance to Alexander Hamilton encourages me to pay some attention to our first poet and his times, causes and failures. As it happens, he too was an antagonist of Alexander Hamilton.

Philip Freneau, the first poet of the United States of America, was also our first professional journalist, encouraged by Thomas Jefferson to edit the *National Gazette,* in which Freneau defended the democratic ideas of Jefferson and James Madison against the elitism and brilliant, aggressive financial projects of Hamilton. Freneau was a shadowed, vulnerable and appealing character. His works and days suggest patterns both inspiring and terrible.

It is possible to describe the career of Captain Freneau, as he was sometimes called, in terms that make it seem glorious and enviable: a life of adventure and accomplishment, art and patriotism, fame and action. He was a soldier, a sailor and a ship's captain, a popular poet of Revolution, a fierce propagandist and editor. His travels included the West Indies, where he witnessed the slave system and wrote memorable poems against it. A few years earlier, he was James Madison's roommate at Princeton, where in 1767 he wrote a commencement ode called "The Rising Glory of America." The revisions of that ode trace a rapid change of psychology from British and colonial to American and revolutionary. Freneau's later political verses and songs became part of the popular culture of the American Revolution, some of them sung aloud in taverns and on battlefields. He fought in the Revolution, first as a member of the New Jersey Militia, taking a bullet in the knee while patrolling the coast between Long Branch and Sandy Hook. Later, as a blockade-runner sneaking supplies to Washington's troops through the inlets of the Jersey coast, he was captured by the British. He survived brutal treatment as a prisoner of war to write patriotic and anti-British poems that had considerable popular impact, reprinted in newspapers all over the new country. He had become "The Poet of the American Revolution." And after the war he became the best known journalistic supporter of Jefferson, of Thomas Paine, and of the ideals of the French Revolution. Jefferson said of him that "he saved our constitution when it was fast galloping into monarchy." And his best non-political poems, in such matters as simplicity of diction, and especially in their treatment of natural detail, seem to anticipate—though written in a raw, provincial culture—the English Romantics of a generation later.

But this life story leaves out the defeat, frustration and misery that dominated Freneau's career. His biographer, Lewis Leary, entitles his book *Philip Freneau: A Study in Literary Failure*. With effective concision, the editors of *The Norton Anthology of American Literature* say of Freneau: "He died impoverished and unknown, lost in a blizzard." Why was Freneau's life so hard and so unhappy, his career so dogged by failure? One answer is that he was an American who deeply loved democracy and poetry, and these loyalties, together and in combination, cooked his goose. They were deeply imprudent passions.

We might expect that a career in poetry would be frustrating, and not immensely remunerative. The other proposition—that an outspoken commitment to democracy could be dangerous to an American of Freneau's day—is perhaps more surprising. It surprised me, when I began looking into his life and reading his work. How good an artist was Freneau? Here is his best-known poem. It is a meditation, in the balanced stanzas of Samuel Johnson's "On the Death of Mr. Robert Levet," on the fact that some Indians bury their dead in a sitting position:

THE INDIAN BURYING GROUND

In spite of all the learned have said,
I still my old opinion keep;
The posture that we give the dead
Points out the soul's eternal sleep.

Not so the ancients of these lands—
The Indian, when from life released,

Again is seated with his friends,
And shares again the joyous feast.

His imaged birds, and painted bowl,
And venison for journey dressed,
Bespeak the nature of the soul,
Activity, that knows no rest.

His bow, for action ready bent,
And arrows with a head of stone,
Can only mean that life is spent,
And not the old ideas gone.

Thou, stranger, that shalt come this way,
No fraud upon the dead commit—
Observe the swelling turf, and say
They do not lie, but here they sit.

Here still a lofty rock remains,
On which the curious eye may trace
(Now wasted, half, by wearing rains)
The fancies of a ruder race.

Here still an aged elm aspires,
Beneath whose far-projecting shade
(And which the shepherd still admires)
The children of the forest played!

There oft a restless Indian queen
(Pale Sheba, with her braided hair)
And many a barbarous form is seen
To chide the man that lingers there.

By midnight moons, o'er moistening dews,
In habit for the chase arrayed,
The hunter still the deer pursues,
The hunter and the deer, a shade!

And long shall timorous fancy see
The painted chief, and pointed spear,
And Reason's self shall bow the knee
To shadows and delusions here.

Clearly, this is in a certain historical manner. Yet the poem is very moving, and not despite its historical manner, and not because we find the historical manner quaint or charming in some condescending way—but in fact partly because the work has mastered and expressed the historical manner, I think indelibly.

This is the very voice of eighteenth-century America: deist and spirit-haunted; grave and tender; striving for balance and restlessly emotional. Trying with this voice as a guide to imagine that time and place, we could start by imagining a New Jersey truly and directly haunted by a displanted race. Freneau could easily look at a Navesink elm tree under which Indian children had played, and that fact gives the poem some of its emotion. This emotion, a mingled guilt and awe, has far more force than the conventional epithets "ruder race" and "barbarous form." It is like the feeling that might have led the tall, fair-skinned invaders who drove the smaller Celts before them into the hills of Britain to invent the fairies or Little People, and it gives the poem some of its mysterious conviction.

Two other elements strike me about the poem. One of these is the ambivalent, questioning and shifting attitude toward matters of the spirit and the supernatural: "the nature of the soul, / Activity, that knows no rest" is in a way a rationalist, eighteenth-century definition, but in another way it is a terrified Romantic vision of the soul as inherently driven, or else a void. And though "life is spent" the old ideas do survive—in a way that is literal or figurative to a carefully unspecified degree. The impressive ghosts of the closing stanzas are treated with a similar delicate ambiguity. At first, the hunter and the deer, the restless queen, the midnight moon, all seem not only shades, but imagined shades, the products of "timorous fancy." But on the other hand they are shadows and delusions to which "Reason's self shall bow the knee": shades, that is, whose real force cannot be denied. It is the language of an agnostic or deist who finds in fear and restlessness themselves a formidable, morally active phantom of old beliefs.

Another striking aspect of the poem is the alternation between language that is effectively formal, such as "In habit for the chase arrayed" which in its balanced syntax and courtly diction gives an eery nobility to its subject, and contrastingly plain, downright language: "They do not lie, but here they sit." Like the oddly memorable, cobbled out opening lines—"I still my old opinion keep"—this note can be called "democratic." To recall the "Lo, the poor Indian" passage in Pope's "Essay on Man" with its generalizing and superior perspective, is to make clear the immediacy and respect in Freneau's handling of physical details: the painted bowl and imaged birds, the bow bent for action and arrows with stone heads. These artifacts get a level closeness of attention distinctly different from the poem's more conventional phrases. To an extent, Freneau put his poem into a voice or idiom that is partly balanced and decorous, and partly homely and American. A similar doubleness has distinguished great American writers—Dickinson and Whitman, Twain and Melville, Frost and Williams—from mere local colorists and mere imitators of European models.

"The Indian Burying Ground" comprehends the claims of imagination, that sees the spear and painted chief, as well as the claims of reason, that shows its respect even while it uses the terms "shadow" and "delusion." Within its conventional language and form, the poem also comprehends both an idiosyncratic American voice and the voice of the European past. If Freneau had managed a whole life's work like this, he might have been our first great poet, as well as our first poet.

Such speculation brings back the subject of Freneau's disastrous worldly career. I think that even his present status as an obscure footnote, perhaps an object for that amused condescension the living accord minor writers, like his nineteenth-century reputation as a disreputable hack, should be seen partly as an extension of that calamitous, headstrong career. And as I have said, the largest part of his problem was his wholehearted aggressive espousal of democracy. Timothy Dwight, president of Yale University, an immensely admired orator and writer, "the most influential religious leader of his time,"[1] grandson of Jonathan Edwards, leading member of the group known as the Connecticut Wits, denounced Freneau as "a mere incendiary, or rather . . . a despicable tool of bigger incendiaries, and his paper a public nuisance." Washington Irving referred

[1] Emory Elliott, *Revolutionary Writers: Literature and Authority in the New Republic, 1725–1810* (Oxford University Press, 1982), p. 56.

to him as "a despicable cur," and George Washington, somewhat more temperately, as "that rascal Freneau."[2]

The issues behind these feelings are remote, yet pertinent, and they involve at its beginnings the question of what a democratic culture—that is, an American life—might be. Even a first look at the issues and figures makes me realize how naive my idea of them has been. The American revolutionaries themselves were naive enough to believe that they would have a country without parties and factions. (Imagine having the runner-up for president serve as vice-president, as in a neighborhood organization.) In practice, social and political forces rapidly created violent factions, and one such force was the Federalist fear, even hatred, of the democratic ideal.

Among Federalist intellectuals, Dwight, the handsome clergyman and college president with the beautiful voice, author of sermons, essays, epic poems, is a suitable figure to contrast with Freneau. Dwight and the other Connecticut Wits disliked democracy, partly on ideological grounds, because it threatened the Puritan New England idea of clerical authority, of Christian ministers controlling the morals and culture of the common people. Egalitarian ideas violated the Calvinist principle of humankind's total depravity; sinners could not govern themselves without an aristocratic clergy. Another, more immediate factor was the fear of the mob and especially the immigrant, Roman Catholic mob. Harrison Gray Otis writes, in 1798, "If some means are not adopted to prevent the indiscriminate admission of wild Irishmen and others to the right of suffrage, there will soon be an end to liberty and property." Vernon Parrington quotes a New England gentleman: "I have seen many, very many Irishmen, and with a few exceptions they are . . . the most God-provoking Democrats on this side of Hell."

So Timothy Dwight hated Jefferson and Freneau because in his eyes democracy meant overturning an established religious, moral and cultural order. Here is Dwight, observing the voting power of moneyless immigrants being drawn off from his home state to the York-state frontier:

---

[2]Vernon Parrington, *Main Currents in American Thought,* vol. 1, *The Colonial Mind 1620–1800* (Harcourt, Brace and World, 1927), pp. 374–75. All subsequent quotations are from Parrington unless indicated otherwise.

[They] are impatient of the restraints of law, religion and morality; grumble about the taxes, by which Rulers, Ministers and Schoolmasters are supported. . . . We have many troubles even now; but we should have many more, if this body of foresters had remained at home.

Rulers, ministers and schoolmasters; grumbling about taxes: this is comical, from one modern perspective, a ludicrous reactionary rage. Underlying it is a sincere, embattled belief in privilege and established authority as the underpinnings of decency and civilization. It is in the context of these convictions that Dwight refers to Freneau as an incendiary.

I don't think an American can easily avoid taking sides in these two-hundred-year-old confrontations. Parrington's characterization of the issues from Freneau's side, counter to the Federalists, is partisan, and stirring:

The source of their disagreement lay in divergences of social philosophy too great to be bridged. In his republicanism Freneau had gone far in advance of the Federalists. He was a democrat while they remained aristocrats. He had rid himself of a host of outworn prejudices, the heritage of an obsolete past, which held them in bondage. He had read more clearly the meaning of the great movement . . . that was shaping a new psychology, and must lead eventually to democratic individualism. He had no wish to stay or thwart that development; he accepted it wholly with all its implications. He had freed his mind from the thralldom of caste. . . . He was an idealist who cared only for the *res publica,* the common well-being, and he desired chiefly that the new government should serve the needs of free people. . . . Like Paine he distrusted all centralizing power. Like Franklin he regarded the everyday world of business and politics as a preposterous arrangement, unconcerned with justice; and he took it on himself to make it over. All his life he was an unmuzzled advocate of whatever new movements gave promise of lessening the old tyrannies. In championing the cause of democracy, he championed a score of lesser causes: Unitarianism, deism, antislavery, Americanism in education: thereby bringing down on his head the resentment of all the conservatisms, religious, political, economic, social, then prospering in America.

The ideas on the other side were also various, in their own way, and extreme. It is hard to realize how very serious the threat of an American monarchy was for Jefferson and his party. (In response, Freneau's persona Peter Slender signed his articles with the attached letters O.S.M.—Order of the Swinish Multitude.)

Freneau's timing for this program could not have been worse. He exhausted himself and made enemies with a newspaper that became famous but never turned a profit. He was out of public life and out of money by the time Jefferson was elected president. They lost his military records, and he couldn't get his pension. He was an old man, and drastically out of style, with his loyalties to the metric of Alexander Pope and to the ideals of the French Revolution, by the time Andrew Jackson took office. American literature surged out beyond his work, and literary history—written, to some extent, by the spiritual heirs of Timothy Dwight and the Federalist intellectuals—slighted him as a gutter fighter, then ignored him.

The struggle between Hamilton and Jefferson can become mythological, the epitome of forces in the national spirit. Comically, Hamilton's genius can seem more abstract than Jefferson's, to some of us, because it has to do with money. It still has the power to shock, as I suppose at some point it shocked Williams. I will try to summarize an example: during the Revolutionary War, patriotic supporters of the Declaration of Independence and the Continental Congress bought bonds to help finance Washington's army. Often, soldiers had been paid in such bonds rather than cash. In the economic circumstances of the times following the war, ordinary people sold these bonds in order to live. Bond prices had fallen, so bonds changed hands at 25 percent or 30 percent of face value, on the general assumption that they would not be redeemed at much more than that. These bonds wound up in the hands of wealthy speculators, mostly in northern commercial cities. (Timothy Dwight was a director of the Eagle Bank, for instance.) Secretary of the Treasury Hamilton's controversial decision was to redeem the bonds at face value, creating tremendous profits for the speculators who had bought them, and securing the "support of property." That is, Hamilton created a class of rich people who would feel patriotic about the United States of America. The bondholders had all the more reason to like the country, and feel a considerable stake in it, because the government immediately exchanged the bonds for new, Federal ones—the country borrowing the face value back from the same holders, and paying them interest on it.[3]

The period can bring out the Ezra Pound in anyone. I couldn't begin to know how necessary such moves by Hamilton were, for the survival of the new Republic. Washington thought they were necessary, and so apparently do many modern historians. This fact does not keep me from sympathizing with Jefferson and Freneau, against Hamilton and Dwight. I will quote from one more poem by Freneau, an effort to write a poem on behalf of liberty. Though it is much less successful than "The Indian Burying Ground" — probably must be called, in the term that haunts Freneau, a failure —the poem has in it plenty to admire, too:

To Sir Toby
    A Sugar Planter in the Interior Parts of Jamaica,
    Near the City of San Jago de la Vega (Spanish Town) 1784

    If there exists a hell—the case is clear—
Sir Toby's slaves enjoy that portion here:
Here are no blazing brimstone lakes—'tis true;
But kindled rum too often burns as blue;
In which some fiend, whom nature must detest,
Steep's Toby's brand, and marks poor Cudjoe's breast.
    Here whips on whips excite perpetual fears,
And mingled howlings vibrate on my ears:
Here nature's plagues abound, to fret and tease,
Snakes, scorpions, despots, lizards, centipedes
No art, no care escapes the busy lash;
All have their dues—and all are paid in cash—
The eternal driver keeps a steady eye
On a black herd, who would his vengeance fly,
But chained, imprisoned, on a burning soil,
For the mean avarice of a tyrant toil!
The lengthy cart whip guards this monster's reign—
And cracks, like pistols, from the fields of cane.
    Ye powers! who formed these wretched tribes, relate,

---

[3]Winthrop D. Jordan, Miriam Greenblatt, and John S. Bowes, *The Americans: The History of a People and a Nation* (McDougal, Littell, 1985), p. 203.

What had they done, to merit such a fate!
Why were they brought from Eboe's sultry waste,
To see that plenty which they must not taste—
Food, which they cannot buy, and dare not steal;
Yams and potatoes—many a scanty meal!—
　　One, with a gibbet wakes his negro's fears,
One to the windmill nails him by the ears;
One keeps his slave in darkened dens, unfed,
One puts the wretch in pickle ere he's dead:
This, from a tree suspends him by the thumbs,
That, from his table grudges even the crumbs!
　　O'er yond rough hills a tribe of females go,
Each with her gourd, her infant, and her hoe;
Scorched by a sun that has no mercy here,
Driven by a devil, whom men call overseer—
In chains, twelve wretches to their labours haste;
Twice twelve I saw, with iron collars graced!—
　　Are such the fruits that spring from vast domains?
Is wealth, thus got, Sir Toby, worth your pains?—
Who would your wealth, on terms like these, possess,
Where all we see is pregnant with distress—
Angola's natives scourged by ruffian hands,
And toil's hard product shipped to foreign lands.
　　Talk not of blossoms, and your endless spring;
What joy, what smile, can scenes of misery bring?
Though Nature, here, has every blessing spread,
Poor is the laborer—and how meanly fed!
　　Here Stygian paintings light and shade renew,
Pictures of hell, that Virgil's pencil drew:
Here, surly Charons make their annual trip,
And ghosts arrive in every Guinea ship,
To find what beasts these western isles afford,
Plutonian scourges and despotic lords:
　　Here, they, of stuff determined to be free,
Must climb the rude cliffs of the Liguanee;
Beyond the clouds, in sculking haste repair,
And hardly safe from brother traitors there.—

It is easy to condemn these lines for their merely competent han-
dling of a style some readers find unsympathetic even at its best: the

style of balanced closed couplets and eighteenth-century epithets. On the other hand, much is reported: the boiling rum, the branding of human flesh, the disease and whippings, the malnutrition, the hangings and ingenious tortures with brine or with nails and wind-mills, the mothers working with hoes in the scorching sun while toting infants. The details are good enough to make Freneau's claim "I saw"—in "Twice twelve I saw, with iron collars graced!"—quite credible. And there are fine moments, even traces of genius in the writing; the literal and living dead blend eerily, for instance, in the lines, "And ghosts arrive in every Guinea ship, / To find what beasts these western isles afford," framed by the references to Virgil's underworld in "Plutonian" and "Charon." In this same passage, "western isles" with its air of exotic beauty makes compactly the point of the earlier, more formal and rhetorical "Talk not of blos-soms, and your endless spring." Moreover, the lines have the force of an intellectual conviction, embodied in the words "of stuff determined to be free," where the two senses of "determined"—subjectively resolute and objectively destined—come together to affirm the idea that freedom is embedded in the stuff of human nature.

Alien though its form and rhetoric are to contemporary taste, "To Sir Toby" resembles some contemporary poetry in its concep-tion. That is, the poem tries to convey a political viewpoint through a vivid catalogue of atrocities. Anyone who has tried to write about such twentieth-century experiences as the bombing of civilian populations, concentration camps, torture of political prisoners, counter-insurgency, the possible nuclear devastation of the globe, has experienced the inevitable recourse to such descriptive catalogue —some subjects, like slavery, seem to demand it—and has felt its problems and limitations. Freneau's poem collapses under these, and it is a collapse important to understand. An explicit account of the failure might be that the Popean rhetorical forms contradict any sense of who addresses the words of the poem to whom. Or, those forms mask the lack of such a sense of whose poem this is. In Pope's list,

> In puns, or politics, or tales, or lies,
> Or spite, or smut, or rhymes, or blasphemies,

the ironically out-of-place element—"rhymes" among smut and blasphemies, "politics," among puns and lies—is like a knowing social joke between reader and writer. The idea of an element that sticks out inappropriately where it seems to strive blandly to belong has everything to do with the aristocratic, melancholy laughter of the "Epistle to Dr. Arbuthnot." Freneau's list, "Snakes, scorpions, despots, lizards, centipedes," frames the term "despots" in the same way, but lamely; there is no place in Freneau's poem for the implied social understanding between him and his reader, the vibration that would animate the twisted parallelism. The truest political component of poetry, the sense of who the poem belongs to, is pale and overpowered by Freneau's enumerated horrors on one side and by his Popean ironies of balance and imbalance, evenness and disproportion on the other side.

Another way to put this is that Freneau's poem "To Sir Toby," skillful in execution and truly admirable in feeling, falls short because it fails to imagine a society—which is to say, an American society—in which the poem itself can take place. In the smaller, elegiac materials of "The Indian Burying Ground," Freneau comes closer to such an imagination. His career is poignant and instructive because it presents an historical extreme. Philip Freneau could write good poems, and he was deeply involved in American life—hard to imagine how anyone could be more deeply involved. He did write good poems, and he wrote popular political ballads and patriotic works. He could write, and he knew America, but he didn't know how to write a poem that situated itself in relation to American life. That challenge has since been met by great poets, and is still with us, I think. The challenge itself wouldn't be articulated for some eighty years.

II

The challenge was articulated by Walt Whitman. "By Blue Ontario's Shore," a poem incorporating much of the 1855 preface to *Leaves of Grass,* displays an ambivalence similar to Williams's rage at the country that "was NOT" great and liberty-loving, "not at all." Whitman's rhapsodic opening section concludes with a negative parenthesis: "(Democracy, the destin'd conqueror, yet treacherous lip-smiles everywhere, / And death and infidelity at every step.)" With Freneau's battles and trials as a background, the embattled, scornful side of Whitman can seem less merely exuberant, more truly threatened and dark.

On the one hand, Whitman disdainfully chastises those who want "only to be told what you knew before," who want "only a book to join you in your nonsense"; and in response to that smugness, he tells us to "Fear grace, elegance, civilization, delicatesse, / Fear the mellow sweet, the sucking of honey juice"—that is, he tells us that, threatened as we are with banality and cliché, only our native vulgarity and freshness will save us. But on the other hand, our native ground contains treachery, lip-smiles, death and infidelity everywhere. And beyond those threats, the very scale and multiplicity of the nation make enormous demands on the bard:

These States are the amplest poem,
Here is not merely a nation but a teeming Nation of nations.

The second line, with its intense emphasis on the plural, qualifies the first one, making it less exalted, and more of a burden for Whitman's American bards. If the heedless, vulgar, fragmented Nation of nations comprises the amplest poem, how does one keep from being swamped by its sheer volume—if not by its death, lip-smiles and infidelity?

The catalogue of the section following "These States are the amplest poem" extends this definition of the tremendous demands which that amplest poem makes of the American poet. He enumerates every aspect of the Americans:

. . . their manners, speech, dress, friendships, the gait they have of persons
who never knew how it felt to stand in the presence of superiors,
The freshness and candor of their physiognomy, the copiousness and decision of their phrenology,
The picturesque looseness of their carriage, their fierceness when wronged

And their habitations and works:

> the fluid movement of the population,
> The superior marine, free commerce, fisheries, whaling, gold
>   digging,
> Wharf-hemm'd cities, railroad and steamboat lines intersecting at
>   all points,

But the catalogue, and this section of "By Blue Ontario's Shore," both conclude at an abrupt, unexpected turn to the negative and conflicted:

> Factories, mercantile life, labor-saving machinery, the Northeast,
>   Southwest,
> Manhattan Firemen, the Yankee swap, southern plantation life,
> Slavery—the murderous, treacherous conspiracy to raise it upon
>   the ruins of all the rest,
> On and on to the grapple with it—Assassin! then your life or ours
>   be the stake, and respite no more.

The unrealized and defective nature of that ample, already overwhelming poem that is the country itself grows out of this ecstatic catalogue in a way both sudden and inevitable: the abrupt, dark side of Whitman. All of the rage, oppression and failure embodied for Whitman by the Civil War, and Lincoln's assassination, concentrate to threaten the mission of the American poet, as well as make that mission urgent.

Whitman, like Freneau generations before, confronted a gulf between ideals of liberty, art, democracy and the actual confusion, provinciality, oppression and economic struggles of American citizens and slaves. Whitman prescribes specifically that these gaps must be closed by poetry:

> I listened to the phantoms by Ontario's shore,
> I heard the voice arising demanding bards,
> By them all native and grand, by them alone can these States
>   be fused into the compact organism of a Nation.

Moreover, he says, "Of all races and eras these States with veins full of poetical stuff most needs poets." The dark side of this famous vision—its pressure and desperation—is almost lost in its audacity, and in how well we know it.

Objectively, what has that vision come to? Does it dwarf our actual poetry? In a way, it is the makers of movies and television, or of American song, who have most vividly fulfilled the Whitmanian vision of fusing the organism of a Nation. However, the medium of poetry is the individual human body. So we can respond on behalf of poetry's peculiar mission that—as Whitman goes on to say—the bard "sees eternity in men and women, he does not see men and women as dreams or dots" (this last word a weird anticipation of the technology of the television screen). Poetry is the art of the individual, what Whitman's next line calls "the great Idea, the idea of perfect and free individuals." "For that, the bard walks in advance."

But linked to poetry's emphasis on the individual voice is another, perhaps even more essential principle. The poet, perhaps more necessarily than the artist in film or the song maker, questions his (or her) art's place in American life, asks all of the questions implied by the conflicts in "By Blue Ontario's Shore." The poet's mission is great in this sense precisely because his place is not sure, not purely indigenous. Whitman establishes the American tradition in which the poet treats American life in his poetry by trying to establish that poetry's place in American life. Whitman does this by raising explicitly, with bravado, the questions that Freneau, in his historical circumstance, cannot begin to frame. To imagine an American life, American poetry characteristically—maybe inevitably—begins by imagining, implicitly or explicitly, its own unrealized place in that life.

No one has seen this more clearly than William Carlos Williams, who wrote this mighty sentence: "It is difficult / to get the news from poems / yet men die miserably every day / for lack / of what is found there." My example of this tradition as it continues into the modern period will be a famous poem by Williams, part XVIII of *Spring and All:*

To Elsie

The pure products of America
go crazy—
mountain folk from Kentucky

or the ribbed north end of
Jersey
with its isolate lakes and

valleys, its deaf-mutes, thieves
old names
and promiscuity between

devil-may-care men who have taken
to railroading
out of sheer lust of adventure—

and young slatterns, bathed
in filth
from Monday to Saturday

to be tricked out that night
with gauds
from imaginations which have no

peasant traditions to give them
character
but flutter and flaunt

sheer rags—succumbing without
emotion
save numbed terror

under some hedge of choke-cherry
or viburnum—
which they cannot express—

unless it be that marriage
perhaps
with a dash of Indian blood

will throw up a girl so desolate
so hemmed round
with disease or murder

that she'll be rescued by an
agent—
reared by the state and

sent out at fifteen to work in
some hard-pressed
house in the suburbs—

some doctor's family, some Elsie—
voluptuous water
expressing with broken

brain the truth about us—
her great
ungainly hips and flopping breasts

addressed to cheap
jewelry
and rich young men with fine eyes

as if the earth under our feet
were
an excrement of some sky

and we degraded prisoners
destined
to hunger until we eat filth

while the imagination strains
after deer
going by fields of goldenrod in

the stifling heat of September
Somehow
it seems to destroy us

It is only in isolate flecks that
something
is given off

No one
to witness
and adjust, no one to drive the car

This perceives the terror of the darkness of American freedom, its
isolation and barrenness: what if freedom from the past, from the

peasant traditions, should leave the imagination not exalted and soaring, but crippled, institutionalized, degraded and feeding on filth? To put it differently, what can a country "purely" of potential become? The poem records Williams first disturbed to feel that the social facts visibly surrounding him indicate a despairing answer: on one side, traditionless gauds and a broken though expressive brain; and on the other, a literally elevated perspective that helplessly views the ribbed valleys from on high, with a vocabulary of "tricked out" and "save numbed terror." The poem moves on and past this point, and through the bleakness of "an excrement of some sky," by finally placing itself at the center of the experience, as an expressive, adjusting witness.

The exhilaration and pain of the poem seem to emanate from the transformed, reiterated word "some": first, as the "some" of arbitrariness that is empty freedom, the meaningless particular—"under some hedge of choke-cherry / or viburnum"; and then later, magnified horribly, in the peculiar and harsh lines, "as if the earth under our feet / were / an excrement of some sky"—the emptiness and degradation of a pastless ground. But in between these two comes the more human scale of "some hard-pressed / house in the suburbs— // some doctor's family, some Elsie." This passage abruptly locates the violent authorial voice, by giving it a social place. By doing that, it marks the turning of the poem from the knowing, sweeping summary and high perspective of the opening lines, toward the resolution of the closing passage, where the straining imagination seems humbled by the uncertainty and possibility of Elsie herself, and the country itself. In these last lines the "some" returns, but a little tempered, in "somehow" and "something." "Somehow" it does seem to destroy us, but on the other hand "something" is given off, in "isolate flecks" that may redeem the hopeless craziness of the "isolate lakes."

The plot of the poem, supported by the changing force of the uncontrolled, unspecifiable, free or crazily random "some," goes from an assertive overview, and literally high perspective, to despair at an immediate social reality, shapeless and voluptuous as water, to a "straining" of the poet's imagination in a "stifling" climate. What can his imagination do in the presence of that overflowing, pastless something, what can it mean? From fitting Elsie into her historical and geographical process, the poem reverses, strains to fit itself, "the imagination," into the context of her life. In this predominantly dark poem, the qualified survival beyond "an excrement," and beyond the "degradation" of prisoners and the destroying of "us," has its root in the qualified optimism of the imagination inventing a daring, rather native image of harmony and guidance—

No one
to witness
and adjust, no one to drive the car

—as if the plain American word "car," and the poem's progress toward it, establish just that minimum understanding or expressiveness demanded. The work that begins trying to include Elsie within the vocabulary of "filth" and "gauds" and "peasant traditions" ends in the final lines by straining for, and arriving at, inclusion within something unexpressed, uncontrolled, both more banal and stranger than the deer going by fields of goldenrod. The effacement or negative mode of the grammatical fragment—*no* one to witness and adjust—makes the imagination's part in the life it would witness the more tentative, the more an open question. In another way, the question is not open: somewhere, somehow, this poem means to witness, to adjust, to drive the car—though not in the visible New Jersey of Elsie and the hard-pressed household. In this poem, and its final image halfway between victory and futility, Williams balances the rage and patriotism he brought to Hamilton, the "great liberty-loving country" and the "vilest swillhole in christendom." He can enclose those warring emotions in his poem by having the poem enclose the effort that made it.

American poetry includes American life by striving to discover poetry's place in American life. Maybe all art does something of the kind, but the pressures involved seem specially American, with our peculiar craziness of cut-off fragments, our jagged purity and desperation, and specially to do with poetry, with its explicitness, its physicality, its sudden, charged evocations of the past, and its power to use the stuff of daily life, the coin of actual discourse and feeling.

II. American Poetry and American Life

When American poetry tries to include American manners it ends by questioning, or trying to assert, its own social place. This questioning, critical and self-critical pull may be one force that drove the Modernist flowering of American poetry in the early twentieth century, making our modern poetry one of the great historical bursts of poetry in English. If the truest political component of poetry is the sense of whom the poem belongs to—the sense of what social manners, assumptions and tastes the poem imagines—modern American poetry has been uniquely situated, between the old, aristocratic authority of the form and against that authority a powerful, shifting social reality. In my own generation, the same force—attention to American life swerving toward attention to the poem's role in that life—seems to impel some of the most valuable work, poems that seem to aim somewhere beyond the sets of mind that imply a settled knowledge of what poetry is and where it belongs: beyond a genial middlebrow tolerance or a bohemian following, an Anglophile mandarin elite or an avant-garde coterie.

If there is any truth in this idea, despite exceptions and qualifications, it can help show what disparate American poems and poets share. For instance, the minor William Carlos Williams poem "Tract," which used to be Williams's main entry in anthologies and textbooks—

> I will teach you my townspeople
> how to perform a funeral—
> for you have it over a troop
> of artists—
> unless one should scour the world—
> you have the ground sense necessary.
> See! the hearse leads.

I begin with a design for a hearse.
For Christ's sake not black—
nor white either—and not polished!
Let it be weathered—like a farm wagon—
with gilt wheels (this could be
applied fresh at small expense)
or no wheels at all:
a rough dray to drag over the ground.

This is not advice, but mock-advice, dramatizing a role the poet does not have. A similar characterization applies to Frank O'Hara's "Ave Maria" ("Mothers of America / let your kids go to the movies! / get them out of the house so they won't know what you're up to"), with its scandalous, unpalatable "they may even be grateful to you / for their first sexual experience / which only cost you a quarter / and didn't upset the peaceful home." In both poems, the point is less the advice than the preposterous quality of the advice, the vacuum that flexes when the poem assumes not only a relation with a communal audience, but the perhaps equally un-likely existence of that audience—as if "my townspeople" or "Mothers of America" had an objective existence as a group, like a feudal manor or the Kiwanis International. Both poems are slight within their author's canons because of this similar, perhaps too self-permissive comedy, the license of a voice that does not matter too much, addressing a phantom gathering.

Here is a brief poem of a nearly opposite kind, that has given many readers pleasure:

Autumn Begins in Martins Ferry, Ohio

In the Shreve High football stadium,
I think of Polacks nursing long beers in Tiltonsville,
And gray faces of Negroes in the blast furnaces at Benwood,
And the ruptured night watchman of Wheeling Steel,
Dreaming of heroes.

All the proud fathers are ashamed to go home.
Their women cluck like starved pullets,
Dying for love.

> Therefore,
> Their sons grow suicidally beautiful
> At the beginning of October,
> And gallop terribly against each other's bodies.

James Wright's poem does not pretend to be addressed to any particular American audience. The convention is not oratorical or mock oratorical, but the lyrical present of "I think." Within that frame, Wright presents the values and strivings of a specific American community, without simply condescending to those values on the one side or giving in to them entirely on the other. With the phrases that end each stanza, he also puts the striving into the context of the epic, European past: "Dreaming of heroes," "Dying for love," "gallop terribly against each other's bodies." Many contemporary poems (and novels and movies) try to include such elements as the place names, the football, the disparity between American working-class life and the idea of freedom.

All this is held together successfully in Wright's poem by the sense of who has made it, who says "I think." The heroic or high language of each stanza's last line is in the first two stanzas partly ironic, because a little limp and bald, the participial fluidity of dreaming of heroes and dying for love. In the last stanza, the qualification is explicit, not ironically implicit: the beautiful young men gallop terribly, and against one another. Who speaks these words? Someone who in the second line "thinks," and with the one appearance of the word "I" uses the low, sometimes offensive expression "Polacks," and who chooses through a grammatical ambiguity to be more or less dreaming of heroes along with the night watchman, and those in the bars and blast furnaces.

The poem's placing of its own utterance takes another turn with the word "therefore," a discursive logical pointer almost parodically different socially from the stadium, bar, steelworks revery of the first movement, and from the declaration of the middle stanza. This rhetorical pointer introduces the third stanza's more heartfelt, successful linking of the local and the heroic—Martins Ferry and the *Iliad*—a linking only yearned-after vaguely by dreams of heroes and dying for love. Linking the local and the heroic is the theme of European poems, too—such as Yeats's "Easter 1916," echoed by "beautiful" and "terribly"; the American element in Wright's poem is embodied by the playing-off of "Polacks" against "therefore," "Tiltonsville" against "heroes" and perhaps even more in the buried, all but lost cultural resonances of American names and phrases. I mean not only the faint ghosts of meaning that vibrate between "shreve" and "high," but the contest between the Germanic and Latin words in the ordinary phrase "football stadium." The very weakness of Classical languages in the American sense of English can give a special overtone to such infinitesimal matters of pitch. And it is matters of pitch that give emotion and meaning to the movement from long beers and blast furnaces to the Homeric image at the end.

In a way, Wright's poem is a meditation on what he has to celebrate, or on the relation between the celebration of poetry and the available glory in American life. What use have the football players or the generations that glory in them for the adverbs and "therefores," the Homeric or chivalric images, of the poet? The variation of idiom, as it threads through poetry's formal demands, puts this question. The play between Latin and Norman roots on one side and Anglo-Saxon roots on the other culminates in the last line's elegant French *galloped*, its normative Latin *terribly*, and blunt Germanic *bodies*. The young men take on both the unconscious beauty of horses and the brutal gallantry of knights. The social criticism that links suicidal beauty and sexual unfulfillment to the drabness and harshness of economic and social conditions may be vague, for some readers even sentimental. But the poem's drama of an authorial "I" who compares his response to this local desire and glory with the old bardic models is precise, clear and beautifully modulated. The poem is opposite in kind to "Tract" and "Ave Maria" because they address patently imaginary audiences disposed to heed poetry, whereas Wright, letting the explicit "I" drop away after his second line, imagines the actual vacuum between the poetry he knows and the America he knows.

The contrast between Latinate and Germanic roots seems to me a characteristically American trope. This is a technical matter that becomes more than a technical matter in the context of an amazing polyglot culture, where high and low, native and imported, lose their old meanings. When Landor exploits this way of varying texture by describing fallen orange blossoms as "crisp" and "unevolved" the contrast appeals to a nineteenth-century British audience that has studied enough Latin in school to hear "evolve" both in its abstract, temporal sense and also in the physical sense of "unroll" or "uncurl." An intuitive, unschooled sense of the difference in texture may miss some of that kind of meaning, but be still more sensitive to others. I mean the intuitive or athletic sense of language that hears the two sources arranged chiastically—home-abroad-abroad-home, or native-Roman-Norman-native—in Jefferson's "Life, Liberty and the Pursuit of Happiness." In that instance, the plain domestic roots "life" and "hap," with their Germanic hominess, bracket the Latin and French overtones of "liberty" and "pursuit" with their flavors of law, the hunt, and books. The rhetoric of the list thus bases the direct, simple needs of "life" and "happiness," beginning and end, in the justifying social atmosphere of monks and lawyers, hunters and knights.

Wallace Stevens may be the American poet who uses this kind of American contrast between "native" and Latin or exotic roots most loudly and overtly—not least by entertaining the idea of French and English as a single language, since each component language would offer more opportunity for contrast, as do his barbaric noises. The noises are a kind of meta-Germanic root, more un-French and therefore more demotic than mere words of any kind could be:

> Poet, be seated at the piano.
> Play the present, its hoo-hoo-hoo,
> Its shoo-shoo-shoo, its ric-a-nic,
> Its envious cachinnation.
>
> If they throw stones upon the roof
> While you practice arpeggios,
> It is because they carry down the stairs
> A body in rags.
> Be seated at the piano.
>
> ("Mozart, 1935")

Arpeggios, stones upon the roof, shoo-shoo-shoo, cachinnation, ric-a-nic and rags: this comic music of widely diverse origins is one music of an American modern that embraces past and present,

Mozart and 1935, and all possible languages—embraces their disparity. The goal of the poet in these lines is the same as in Stevens's "The American Sublime": to "confront the mockers, / The mickey mockers"—words which make a similar native music out of the Latinate verb *confront* and the English object *mockers,* the verb corresponding to the poet and the object to the mocking laughter —the derisory cachinnation—of his fellow Americans.

Some other examples: The title of "An Ordinary Evening in New Haven" uses in the first word after the article an exotic root (with echoes of church government) to denote the idea of routine, echoed by the Germanic second word with its similar meaning— "making things even"—so that these two words together may perhaps by contrast awaken just a little of the sense of freshness and hazard sleeping in the last two: new, haven. "A single voice," as the poem itself says more clangorously, using the verbal noises, the exotic word, the contrasted roots, to make a diverse music, held together by a comic unity in discord: past and present, exotic and domestic, Europe and America, all joined in what the poet chooses to say:

> A celestial mode is paramount,
> If only in the branches sweeping in the rain:
> The two romanzas, the distant and the near,
> Are a single voice in the boo-ha of the wind.

When Stevens reaches toward the eclectic sounds of American names, which are not American in their parts but only in the process of their making—"Mrs. Alfred Uruguay," "Cortège for Rosenbloom"—the effect is to locate his imagination between a foreign element and a less foreign, the distant and the near, the poet more than a little on guard defining his own place by incorporating the widest possible range of contrasts. The comic beauty of disproportionate parts gives a role to the poet who combines them. By incorporating the vulgar laughter, by calling it "cachinnation," he asserts his place in relation to it.

This is not anyone's favorite side of Stevens. It reminds us of his limitations, it has the quality of snobbery, the pathos and fearfulness that mickey mockers will find in his music only a laughable dandyism. On the other hand, the energy that enables his great poems seems to come partly from this need to question and adjust his place, to confront the comedy of that quest by exaggeration. And however mannered or arch, his collisions and noises reflect an American eclecticism of culture, the not-quite melting pot of imports and appropriations. By exaggerating the strangeness and odd yokings in the national language, he dramatizes the strange and yet oddly indigenous nature of his work.

Here is an example of a somewhat similar effect from an extremely dissimilar direction, the opening stanzas of Jean Toomer's "Georgia Dusk":

The sky, lazily disdaining to pursue
    The setting sun, too indolent to hold
    A lengthened tournament for flashing gold,
Passively darkens for night's barbecue,

A feast of moon and men and barking hounds,
    An orgy for some genius of the South
    With blood-hot eyes and cane-lipped scented mouth,
Surprised in making folksongs from soul sounds.

The sawmill blows its whistle, buzz-saws stop,
    And silence breaks the bud of knoll and hill,
    Soft settling pollen where plowed lands fulfill
Their early promise of a bumper crop.

Smoke from the pyramidal sawdust pile
    Curls up, blue ghosts of trees, tarrying low
    Where only chips and stumps are left to show
The solid proof of former domicile.

Toomer's sunset lets the Tennysonian "lengthened tournament for flashing gold" clang against the deeply native word *barbecue* (an Indian word taken into Spanish and French). The idiom of the poem associates that contrast between old richness and new, European and American, exotic and plain, with the contrast between kinds of root, the alternated "lazily" and "disdaining," "indolent" and "hold," "passively" and "darkens," all complicated and folded back by exotic "barbecue" coming from Indian through Romance languages to play against plain Germanic "night." The effect is less like Stevens than like Hart Crane, the richness of old pentameter eloquence made richer by the untamed, cane-lipped genius of the specific American place, the sexual, heavily atmospheric silence that settles, in a brilliant image, like pollen. It is an atmosphere that teases and questions the poet's own voice: who says "barbecue" in the rhythms of Tennysonian quatrains and sunsets, against that sexual Georgia silence? By implication, the poem wonders what human voice or voices can put "bumper crop" and "domicile" together in this place where landscape and human life both seem to evade the poet's terms.

The poem's rhythms, the closed pentameter quatrains, seem to slow and stall as the pollen of fading light and quieted machinery settles over it: "Surprised in making folksongs from soul sounds." The spondaic phrase of "soul sounds" and the term "folksongs" stall and drawl in a kind of loving self-mockery. The rest of the poem converts the implicit comparison of song and poem into explicit action:

Meanwhile, the men, with vestiges of pomp,
　　Race memories of king and caravan,
　　High-priests, an ostrich, and a juju-man,
Go singing through the footpaths of the swamp.

Their voices rise . . the pine trees are guitars,
　　Strumming, pine-needles fall like sheets of rain . .
　　Their voices rise . . the chorus of the cane
Is caroling a vesper to the stars . .

O singers, resinous and soft your songs
　　Above the sacred whisper of the pines,
　　Give virgin lips to cornfield concubines,
Bring dreams of Christ to dusky cane-lipped throngs.

With this vivid, culturally mixed, many-rooted procession the simple alternation of roots breaks into a multiple fracturing and re-blending of linguistic elements—Arabic and Latin, African and

English, *juju-man* and *king, swamp* and *caravan, pine* and *guitar, strummings* and *vespers* of the *cane.*

These singing voices have an assurance and unity unlike that of the poem that describes them; the singers give no sign that they find their pomp "vestigial," nor does their singing seem to encompass anything like the tension between pentameter stanzas and high diction on one hand and juju-man, barbecue and landscape on the other. On the contrary: "Their voices rise . . the chorus of the cane." Witnessing the singers, Toomer by implication compares his work to theirs, a comparison marked by a return, in the final stanza, from the multiple roots that evoke the procession back to the alternating pattern of Latin and Germanic: *resinous* and *soft, sacred* and *whisper;* and in the perfect chiasmus of the next-to-last line:

Give virgin lips to cornfield concubines,

where the opposed Latin conceptual terms for the female body frame the earthbound *lips* and *cornfield.* As if bursting out of this intellectual bracketing, the monosyllabic, physical terms win out in the final line's imperative: "Bring dreams of Christ" and "dusky cane-lipped throngs" jamming the movement to a Hopkins-like retard, echoing the earlier "making folksongs from soul sounds." Whether this imperative is based on the actual weaving of Christian hymns into a partly African ritual, or imagines it, the poem's final plea or prayer is to have its own contradictory roots and intentions made coherent. The bringing together of Christianity and the culture visible in the cornfield is no more or less fantastic than the bringing together of this American scene with what the poet brings to the scene. The poem, reaching for a mystic eloquence similar to that which Crane was fashioning at the same time, ends by calling up a paradoxical, visionary idea of coherence.

This American version of "The Solitary Reaper," in other words, expresses its action partly through a kind of formal inclusion of many actual and potential voices. The somewhat cumbersome technical term might be formal heteroglossia. Each moment of idiom and rhythm asks what tongue should speak next—what language, what person, in what cadence? (From this perspective, the Black poets of the nineteenth and early twentieth century are not fringe elements in the record of our poetry, but characteristic, even quintessential, insofar as the clash between means and experience may require an American poet to forge imaginatively his own place in what he sees.)

The questioning demanded by our heterogeneous life finds its expression in heteroglossia. American poetry's exploitation of the English language's immense and bastardized vocabulary, including the abstraction and formality tied to Latinate words, the physicality and plainness of Germanic words, is only one example of such sensitive mixing and blending. The American poet's relation to levels of syntax, or to kinds of lore and learning, breaking and rearranging ideas of high and low, might offer other examples. This way of looking at style is another way to see the association between modernism and American art. The rapid, shifting play between formality and informality; movement between traditional rhythm and its breaking, and back; levels of syntax speeding ambiguously up and down and through "spoken" constructions and "written" ones; syntax racing or drifting through resemblance to innumerable kinds of speech, kinds of writing—these and all of the other kinds of flexibility and speed one might call "Modernist" are also responses to American social reality, especially if one thinks of that reality as one where poetry itself may be an alien or unrealized presence.

As I have tried to suggest by looking at Toomer's poem and some lines of Stevens, such mixing and testing—"formal heteroglossia" —characterizes our poetry over a wide range of different concerns and styles. For instance, an athletic sureness in finding an idiom and form adequate to such thrilling, shifting ground characterizes both Robert Frost and William Carlos Williams, a quality they share under their differences. Whether it is sentences shooting with unexpected grace and knots through iambic channels, or the syncopation of free verse, what we admire in both poets is a formal resourcefulness in defining one's place on shifting ground. Their work brings the speech and behavior of their American social setting into an energetic, self-calibrating struggle with all that poetry was, just before they came to it. In comparison, no matter how active and jagged the imagination of W. H. Auden may be, the enclosing idiom and form that indicate the social frame of his work seem relatively fixed and solid.

Another kind of contrast with the work of Frost and Williams might be a mere regionalism: place as an end rather than a means, the imaginative re-creation, contrary to fact, of stable ground: New Jersey or New England presented as if without the contradiction and movement embodied by their very names. And yet the contradiction and movement of national life as a whole can in some ways be responded to only through a region or place, New Haven or Georgia, the particular names and features flashing by in their change and ambiguity like the distance markers in a car race. There is a comic relish to this process, ebulliently invoking a place almost to doubt its moral reality or permanence, as in Philip Levine's poem "An Ordinary Morning," which begins, "A man is singing on the bus / coming in from Toledo." The man and the bus driver sing to one another, like bizarrely transformed shepherds out of Spenser or Sidney, about love and about the new day, as the passengers wake up, watery-eyed. Levine's closing lines characteristically mix notes and keys—high and low, comic and exalted, local and global, ironic and heartfelt:

> The sun enters from a cloud
> and shatters the wide windshield
> into seventeen distinct shades
> of yellow and fire, the brakes
> gasp and take hold, and we are
> the living, newly arrived
> in Detroit, city of dreams,
> each on his own black throne.

To take just a few examples: "the sun enters" is both a comic stage direction, and a heroic substitute for the ordinary "the sun comes out." The literal shattering of the windshield in one line is revealed in the next as figurative, and that line in turn with its "seventeen" shades is both extravagantly descriptive and slangy. The enjambed lines imitate this same changing or combining of tones, lifting or dropping: "shades" turned by "of yellow and fire" toward violence and energy; "brakes" turned by "gasp" toward human wonder and back from the mundane; "the living" widening the range of "we are" while maybe dropping its tone back toward the mundane; "newly arrived," which suggests new birth after "the living," drops back comically with "in Detroit." And "the living, newly arrived / in Detroit, city of dreams" is not entirely ironic. The history of Detroit as a place where whites and blacks went from the rural South to work in automobile plants is certainly a history of dreams, a history as ambiguous as the final image of the poet and other bus riders, "each on his own black throne." One could exemplify this fluidity of tone, including the inseparable blend of comic and ecstatic, formal and vulgar, in an enormous range of American poets, John Ashbery and Elizabeth Bishop, George Oppen and James Merrill, Allen Ginsberg and Marianne Moore. (I think that the stylistic trait I mean also characterizes poems that do not explicitly take up American cultural material such as bus rides or movies.)

I have been trying to describe modern American poetry's capacity for formal surprise, a sense of mystery about how a thing will be uttered. Beginning with the first modernist generation, the social aspect of this surprise and indeterminacy has been accompanied by another, philosophical aspect, a preoccupation with the unreliability or rigidity of language itself. In my own generation, these elements have taken on new configurations, in works that criticism has hardly begun to catch up with or identify. I mean, for instance, the fluidity of the transitions in James McMichael's *Four Good Things,* a book-length poem set in Pasadena, where Cal Tech was first founded as a crafts school in the spirit of William Morris: the way McMichael moves from his stamp collection through an analysis of the styles of British and German imperialism, through the wind tunnel and the first experiments with television and the beams of cathode-ray electrons, synchronized each thirtieth of a second ("successively, in league, they looked like something")—the whole movement of twenty or thirty lines alluding to countless levels of speech, as it drifts toward, and then far away from, iambic pentameter. The range of McMichael's book, and its formal fluidity, embody an art that defies any trite social correlatives of form, the conservative sestina or liberated free verse. Every line he writes includes some formal twist, or some surprising, rapid verbal turn, that confounds such categories.

I'll try to show what I mean by looking in some detail at another recent poem. Here are the first four stanzas of Anne Winters's "Night Wash":

> All seas are seas in the moon to these
> lonely and full of light.
> High above laundries and rooftops
> the pinstriped silhouettes speak nightmare
> as do the faces full of fire and orange peel.
> Every citizen knows what's the trouble: *America's longest*
> *river is—New York: that's what they say, and I say so.*
>
> Wonderful thing, electricity,
> all these neons and nylons spun dry by a dime
> in the Fifth Street Laundromat. The city
> must be flying a thousand kites tonight
> with its thousands of different keys.
> —Sir, excuse me, *sir?*
> Excuse me interfering, but you don't want
> to put that in—it's got a rubber backing, see? Oh, not at
>   all . . .
>
> Piles of workshirts, piles of leopard underthings,
> it's like fishing upside down all night long, and then the moon
>   rises
> like armfuls of thready sleeves. Her voice
> rising and falling, her boys folded sideways asleep on the bench:
> —Listen, that old West Indian cleaning lady?
> Ask anyone here, she never has change.
> Come on, she's too wise . . .
>
> Down in the Tombs
> the prisoner's knuckles climb like stripes
> of paint in the light. He dreams he hears
> the voice of a pig he used to slop for his uncles.
> It pokes its head
> through the bars and says
> "Have you brought any beet greens?"

One interesting thing about the passage is its mixture of the literary and the colloquial, or rather several kinds and degrees of the literary and the colloquial. These are innumerable: the formal, rather dense and elevated first sentence, the written language of poetry; the plainer, more spoken poetry of the sentence about neons and nylons; the italicized, spoken but rather formal sentence about New York as our longest river; the somewhat stiff speech, possibly the poet's, in the actual dialogue, "Excuse me interfering"; the other voice that talks about the cleaning woman; the omniscient sentence that knows what the prisoners dream in the Tombs; the more limited sentence that sees the children folded sideways like laundry; the slight primness of saying "underthings"; the voice that dreams; the voice of the pig. . . . The chorus of silent and uttered and dreamed sentences, formed and unformed voices, is the sound of the long river that is the city. Someone has uncles; someone makes the fanciful simile about fishing upside down all night long; someone makes an allusion to Benjamin Franklin's experiment with electricity; and it is not the fragmentation but the flow, the dreamy and resistless movement from part to part, moment to moment, that carries much of the developing emotion.

Without the sense of motion and merging, the details might seem merely rich, imaginatively conceived or recorded. Instead, they suggest a restless demand, a congeries of needs floating and drowning, and so prepare for the next movement of the poem with its images of water:

> —You can never leave them alone at night. Like today
> the stitching overseer says to me
> If you can't keep the rhythm missus . . .
> I says to him fire
> me all you want, I don't take that shit
> off anybody. That was a scare though—
> you can't always get back on a day shift.

> In the moonlight
> the city rides serenely enough, its thousand light moorings
> the hunted news in their eyes. Even the rivers
> are tidal, as sailors and bankers know.
> The glass bank of the Chase Manhattan stands dark
> over the Harbor. One last
> light slowly moving around the top floor.

The bizarre wit that sees the building of the financial bank as a harbor bank floats almost innocuously and tonelessly in its surroundings; the light moves like a boat around the bank above the capitalized microcosm of the Harbor. Then this dream world yields to the focus of dialogue or monologue again, and the conclusion:

> —No washing machines in the basement, that's
> what's the trouble. The laundry would dry overnight
> on the roof, in the wind. Well a month ago
> you know, some big boys took this twelveyearold
> little Spanish girl up there. Then they killed her, they
> threw her, six stories down. Listen, the stone age or something
> running around on those roofs. So this cop said to me
> *Your street is the bottom,* he actually
> said that to me. So what could I say—that it's great?
>
> On the folding table the same
> gestures repeat, smoothing and folding
> the same ancient shirt. Or the old West Indian cleaning lady
> pretending to finger her pockets for change. At midnight she'll
>   prop
> her gray spaghetti mop and glide toward you
> in her black cotton trousers, her black
> lavender face tilted up. Very clearly
> she says to the world in dream-language
> *I mean to live.*

"They killed her" and "they threw her" have the more force because of the sleepy sentence fragments like "One last / light slowly moving around the top floor" and "No washing machines in the basement, that's / what's the trouble." Characteristically, one of these two fragments is in the framing narrative voice while the other is spoken by a character, a character whose remarks have a skewed moral conviction: "that's / what's the trouble," "he actually / said that to me." The fragments and the certainty bob in the aqueous world of the poem along with the muted ordinary street comedy of "stone age or something," "the bottom," "it's great."

Fragments, two of them, begin the last stanza as well, followed by the peculiar sequence of tenses, future ("At midnight she'll prop") then present ("she says"). This is the sequence of prophecy or vision, but then again one of my favorite notes in the last stanza is the way the homely phrase "spaghetti mop" comes in, heightening the drugged or dream quality, with its odd rhyme on "prop." "Ancient" and "stone age" belong here along with the mop, and along with the last recurrence of the prim or stiff diction, on "trousers." My terms—note, voice—are the best I can do in tracing the open, uncentered but clear movement that places the horror of the child's death in its true, placeless or flowing locale. The poem's last phrase, the italicized *"I mean to live,"* spoken in a language that the poem identifies as no language of this waking earth, also sounds like the language of a definite person in a place, so that we can believe the authorial "very clearly." The two senses of the verb *mean* as "I intend to live" and "I signify living" come together very clearly, in the final phrase that confirms and summarizes the poem's movement. That movement, the way each moment in the poem's course means to live, conveys its emotion, where a lesser poem might try merely to deplore or exploit. I think that Winters's mastery of an extreme, packed formal alertness is part of a characteristically American response to shifting, undetermined manners, forms and idioms, to heroic structures and appalling lives and deaths.

To put it differently, I like the visible speed and intelligence of Anne Winters's poem. These qualities don't necessarily depend upon the direct treatment of social details and materials—I don't intend anything as quixotic or odious as prescribing a subject matter, or proscribing one. Rather, the point is that a certain kind of fluidity, a formal and moral quality, seems to have been demanded of American poets by their circumstance: in some ways, having to do with expectation and need, poets are at the center of national life, where Whitman would have them; in other ways they are at the fringes, supplanted by the overwhelming variety and power of a reckless national culture.

Fluidity and rapidity have a lot to do with what I like about poetry itself. The mind in it glides and whirls like an ice skater over its medium; prose often wades. Some of the effortful straining of experimental fiction seems to struggle for poetry's freedom to dart from narrative to meditation to exposition and back, inserting a self-reflexive undermining of narrative illusion and then restoring narrative again, without visible seams or audible creaks. It seems possible that such motion is redoubled in the modern American context. Philosophical worrying at the nature of language itself, which has characterized modernism from its beginnings, becomes ever more conventional, an historical gesture. The open question of America's use for poetry refreshes that gesture, gives it a perpetually renewed meaning. Winters's laundromat with its *"I mean to live"* seems simultaneously to challenge and embarrass poetic language, and to incorporate it: to defy poetic form, and to demand it. Language itself may be untrustworthy; the language we use here is also immense, strangely broken, unforeseeable.

I have tried to suggest that American poetry's critical response to American life has been inherently a self-criticism as well: the disparate, mutually revising phrases "I don't take that shit / off anybody" and the "thousand light moorings" take their place in the endless debate between pairs like Toomer's "barbecue" and "pyramidal" or Stevens's "arpeggio" and "shoo-shoo-shoo," each pair with its dreamy aspiration and its saving vulgarity. This conflict is a special, American version of the old contest between all of established rhetoric on one side and the fresh growths of culture and personal experience on the other. To paraphrase Yeats's distinction between poetry and rhetoric, it is American poetry's ongoing argument with itself. Literary criticism has hardly begun to trace the sinuous course of that debate, and the formal means that embody it, in American poetry since the modernist generation.

This self-examination is not necessarily a dour, embattled process. I have in mind something more like the closing lines of Frank O'Hara's "Naphtha," with its brilliant collage of the Eiffel Tower, where Jean Dubuffet did his military service as a meteorologist; New York's Iroquois construction workers "unflinching-footed" on steel girders high over the city; Duke Ellington; the American Century's technological nightmares, wars and works of art. At the end O'Hara says: "I am ashamed of my century / for being so entertaining / but I have to smile." By finishing off his eclectic and eccentric catalogue with a happy, nearly apologetic reflection on his own response, the poet acknowledges his unsettled role. It is a moment that reminds me, in its sudden, cheerful confession of a not-yet-settled subjectivity, of Williams spiralling from "The pure products of America" to "some doctor's family, some Elsie." On the one hand, the poet is alone and must be one; on the other hand, the many-voiced mode, the poem implying more voices than we can see or hear, let alone identify, seems the only means suited for such vast quantities and qualities of shame and entertainment. The question of who speaks or writes and the question of what kind of many-voiced place that one speaker or writer inhabits become one question.

III

SALT WATER

Salt Water

All four of my grandparents came to live in Long Branch, New Jersey, when they were young. Long Branch is an ocean resort, once a famous watering spot painted by Winslow Homer, visited by Abraham Lincoln and Diamond Jim Brady: "the Newport of its day," people said. But in the days when my grandparents raised their families in Long Branch, and later when I grew up there, the town was decayed: the beach eroded, the boardwalk on the famous bluffs given over to honky-tonk, many of the immense Victorian "cottages" on Ocean Avenue converted to hotels or to "cook-alones" or gutted by Jewish Lightning, as arson for insurance purposes was known.

I have an early memory of going down to the ocean in a car to watch a hurricane. From across the boardwalk, through sheets of rain, feeling the car rock on its springs in the mighty gusts, we saw the water spill in exhilarating sheets over the seawall, submerge the jetties and break off chunks of pavement and boardwalk. As a climax, the hurricane that year tore a hot dog stand right off its wooden stilts and into the ocean.

Except for one unhappy year in Chicago, I have always lived near salt water; so have my brother and sister and cousins. My grandfather Dave Pinsky was among other things a bootlegger during Prohibition; since one or two of the family stories from those days involve boats, the ocean may have had a practical, commercial importance to him. But it is not easy to picture him with the spray in his face, or even with his clothes wet. He is a figure from *Roaring Twenties,* not *Man of Aran.* He was a professional fighter for a time, and there is a picture of him in a black turtle neck, scowling and putting up his fists in the traditional pose.

His raffish, rowdy confidence has always appealed to me. Grandpa Dave, with his bar (the Broadway Tavern), his big hands and ape face, his gentile wife (number three) and his enormous Christmas tree, exerted a thuggish swank, an attractive counterforce away from another conception of being Jewish, a cerebral timidity epitomized by debate about Christmas carols. Should Jewish kids in public school sing them as "just songs"? A boy called Barney Hirsch took the opposite view that one must stand mute and immobile. Some compromisers lip-synched without vocalizing, while others omitted the religious parts only:

La-la the Savior is born!

The point about Grandpa Dave was not assimilation, but something like assurance.

It was partly a small-town assurance. The bar and his past made him firmly a local character. My father, an optician rather than a barkeeper, had a certain small-town outlook as well. I can hear him asking me, about an encounter with a teacher, storekeeper, cop, doctor: "Did he know who you were?" This wasn't said with arrogance, but with respect for the idea that we fit in the fabric of the place. The other side of the question was something like: "I know who he is; his uncle is an asphalt contractor. He used to do a specialty number at dance marathons."

This small-town element, and a kind of criminal element, and what I'll call the salt-water element, have seemed left out, to me, in many American novels about Jewish life in New York or Chicago. I am tempted to distinguish between New York Jews and salt-water Jews. This may explain why I love Isaac Babel's Odessa stories, with their romanticized Jewish gangsters:

Reb Arye-Leib was silent, sitting on the cemetery wall. Finally he said:

"Why he? Why not they, you wish to know? Then see here, forget for a while that you have spectacles on your nose and autumn in your heart. Cease playing the rowdy at your desk and stammering while others are about. Imagine for a moment that you play the rowdy in public places and stammer on paper. You are a tiger, you are a lion, you are a cat. You can spend the night with a Russian woman, and satisfy her. You are twenty-five. If rings were fastened to heaven and earth, you would grasp them and draw heaven and earth together. . . . That's why he's the King, while you thumb your nose in the privy."

And then the old man tells the youth the comical epic tale of Benya's rise to become king of the dockside gangsters. One of the many things that interest me in the quotation is the process of mythologizing and glamorizing. I recognize that process, independently of content. (And Odessa is, of course, a seaport.) I recognize the scene of the old man telling the youth a story that he probably knows already.

One of the main junkyards in Long Branch used to belong to a man called, oddly enough, Ash. I went to Izzy Ash's junkyard in the summer of 1962 to get a part for a 1953 Dodge convertible which I proposed to drive out to California. I was going to be a poet, and I was going to Stanford. Mr. Ash took this in as he grunted and tugged at a long-handled wrench, removing the part I needed from a wrecked Coronet.

I told Mr. Ash that I was going to graduate school, not that I was going to be a writer. As it happens, he knew more than might be expected about going to graduate school. And I had already, that summer, been embarrassed by the idea that I was a writer.

A Long Branch boy called Danny Pingitore was having some minor success under another name as a television actor at this time. The absurdity of the ambitions I was carrying West with me had been driven home when Danny phoned me earlier that summer. I didn't really know him, he was at least five years older than I was, but our mothers had run into one another in a store, and he was in Long Branch for part of July.

"Robert, this is Danny Pingitore. Your mother says you are going out to California to be a writer."

"Well, yes."

"There's something I really want to tell you."

"What's that?"

"Don't go."

"What?"

"Don't go, Robert, I mean it. I know a lot of writers in L.A. and they all say this is the worst year for it. It was okay for a while, but they aren't producing any more hour shows at all. Everything is half-hour shows. That's all they're making, and most of the writers out there already can't get work."

So I simply told Mr. Ash that I was going to Stanford, to graduate school. In Izzy Ash's class at Long Branch High School there were two outstanding students, both from Jewish families. Both went to Harvard: Mike Abrams and Barry Green, two brilliant and ambitious Long Branch boys whose stories still meant something to Mr. Ash as he braced his feet against the sandy, shadeless, oil-stained dirt of his junkyard and pulled a part free along its channeled bracket. He had his generation's respect for what doing well in school could do for somebody whose family had no money or power. So he told me about Mike and Barry.

Mike Abrams went from Harvard College to graduate school and became a distinguished professor, the author of a famous book (*The Mirror and the Lamp,* a study of the two Romantic images for poetry; though I had not exactly read it, I knew that it was—as it did prove to be—very good). Barry Green became a rich, clever lawyer, but sadly—as Mr. Ash told me the story he knew I knew —in the course of his climb to success he got in deep with the Mob, including a deal that involved selling orange peels to the government for the production of synthetic sugar. The deal was saturated in fraud, bribery, chicanery—even, when you think about it, despoiling the Treasury in wartime; and the dukes and generals of the Mob (in Long Branch, where Vito Genovese had his once-famous yellow eyeglasses made by my father, "Mafia" always sounded almost highbrow or literary), protecting the myth of their patriotism, declared that Barry Green would have to go to prison, and so he did. The alternative was testifying, and sudden disappearance. His wife and daughters—both beautiful, they took elocution lessons, and the younger one was the first girl in town to play Little League—were taken care of by the dukes.

Meanwhile, the story concluded, Mike Abrams continued the idyllic life of an honored professor at Cornell University, an Ivy League college in a class with Harvard itself.

Mr. Ash sighed emphatically. He knew from his children, my classmates, that I had not been a good student in high school, and his telling me this story was a way of indicating respect for my new seriousness. Wiping his head with his forearm, he finished with a moral:

"Yes, Robert, there's two different paths in life: it's just like North Broadway and South Broadway."

Having said this, Izzy Ash held out to me the extracted, rebuildable fuel pump of the Coronet. Broadway's two forks, North and South, form a Y just a couple of blocks from the beach. One of the things that seemed funny to me about Mr. Ash's allegorizing of the town, even as I nodded solemnly, is that North Broadway and South Broadway extend only to arrive at exactly the same place— the Atlantic Ocean.

On Broadway not far from where it divides there was a string of Jewish-owned businesses; those shops produced a number of distinguished names. One—was it a paint and hardware store?— belonged to the parents of M. H. Abrams. Norman Mailer's aunt had a dress shop called, I think, Estelle's. Another store of some kind paid for the first lessons of the noted pianist Julius Katchen. And I think that the parents of Jeff Chandler, the movie star who played Cochise in *Broken Arrow,* owned the delicatessen. Their name was Grossel.

The feeling about a place that makes people pass on such lore— I probably have the details all wrong, but those people really were born in Long Branch—is a feeling of importance. To mythologize or inflate a community, or even to make anecdote (or allegory) of it, is both to submerge one's identity partway into the communal identity, and to assert one's importance. To make one's native place illustrious is an acceptable, ancient form of claiming personal significance. As a kind of impersonal boasting, it raises the great conflict and accommodation between self and community, figure and background.

The sense of importance, or heroic weight, is a big part of what thrills me in Edwin Arlington Robinson's "Eros Turannos," the power of the plural *we* and the way that uncomprehending, smugly provincial *we* vibrates and gives a greater power to the singular *her,* in the closing stanzas:

The falling leaf inaugurates
  The reign of her confusion;
The pounding wave reverberates
  The dirge of her illusion;
And home, where passion lived and died,

Becomes a place where she can hide,
While all the town and harbor side
   Vibrate with her seclusion.

We tell you, tapping on our brows,
   The story as it should be,—
As if the story of a house
   Were told, or ever could be;
We'll have no kindly veil between
Her visions and those we have seen,—
As if we guessed what hers have been,
   Or what they are or would be.

Meanwhile we do no harm; for they
   That with a god have striven,
Not hearing much of what we say,
   Take what the god has given;
Though like waves breaking it may be,
Or like a changed familiar tree,
Or like a stairway to the sea
   Where down the blind are driven.

The excitement of this gloomy grandeur and glory—"they / That with a god have striven"—depends upon the peculiar relationship between the rather mean-minded, brow-tapping townfolk and the woman. Though she does not hear much of what they say, they help give her isolation heroic scale, as surely as she gives them something worth talking about.

This relationship of the tragic individual to the provincial community comes through so powerfully that it almost obliterates the equally brilliant first half of the poem, where the woman's choice of a terrible love affair over no love at all is etched with enormous conviction. The poem is charged with all the pride and frustration Robinson must have felt as a penniless, ailing provincial, successful neither in the terms of small-town life nor in the terms of the standard literary culture of the 1890s and after, whose magazines wanted no part of his work.

I think I love the poem partly for the detail that Long Branch shares with the Maine town Robinson was thinking of—the "stairway to the sea." And just as large, spooky vibrations course between "her" and "we," other tremendous, old forces pass between the Homeric opposites "sea" and "home":

> And home, where passion lived and died,
> Becomes a place where she can hide,
> While all the town and harbor side
>   Vibrate with her seclusion.

Her house is near the ocean, and her home town, where we think we know so much, is right on the ocean. Stairs go right down to where the waves crash. Her fate and glory, her *doom* in the original sense, all seem located out there, in the same dangerous, productive waters where the swarthy, piratical sea-trading businessmen who made a first ideal audience for *The Odyssey* located glory, death, wonder and profit. Telemachos is set out onto it in order to make a name for himself. "Home" and "sea," being of a place and leaving it: Robinson's poem makes Izzy Ash seem less ludicrous, more an intuitively bardlike figure. Only Harvard, Hollywood, New York seem inadequate to their half of the Homeric equation. Broadway, with its two forks and its ambitious, cunning sons, seems Ithaca enough, when one reads Robinson's poem.

In Babel's story "Awakening," the Jewish fathers of Odessa run a "lottery, building it on the bones of little children." That is, since Mischa Elman and Jascha Heifetz were Odessa babies, all of the kids in that circle were taught music, by Mr. Zagursky, who ran "a factory of Jewish dwarfs in lace collars and patent-leather pumps," girls "aflame with hysteria" pressing violins to their "feeble knees," "big-headed, freckled children with necks as thin as flower stalks and an epileptic flush on their cheeks."

The narrator, at fourteen, is beyond "the age limit set for infant prodigies," but he is short and weak, as small as an eight-year-old: "Herein lay my father's hope." The father, significantly, is hopelessly and insanely obsessed not with money but with glory: "though my father could have reconciled himself to poverty, fame he must have."

But the boy props a book by Turgenev or Dumas on the music stand, while "the sounds dripped from my fiddle like iron filings, causing even me excruciating agony." And one day, on the way to Zagursky's for a lesson, the boy sets out on his own course for glory.

He begins secretly cutting the lessons and heads in another direction, the direction in which Athene tells Telemachos to seek glory in Book One of the Odyssey. He heads for the ocean.

Down by the docks, he accompanies his friend Nemanov onto an English ship to get a consignment of smuggled handmade pipes. (The boy Nemanov will grow up to find glory as "a New York millionaire, director of General Motors, a company no less powerful than Ford.") Torn in "a struggle of Rabbis versus Neptune," the would-be writer, on one of these days by the docks, meets an old man who teaches him how to swim, encourages him as a writer, and commands him to look for the first time at the natural world. ("In my childhood, chained to the Gemara, I had led the life of a sage. When I grew up I started climbing trees.") As Babel puts it, "the local water-god took pity on me."

This water-god, proofreader of the *Odessa News,* reads a work of the boy's, "a tragedy I had written the day before." The old man reads, runs a hand through his hair, paces up and down; then—

"One must suppose," he said slowly, pausing after each word, "one must suppose that there's a spark of the divine fire in you."

The water-god then immediately takes the boy outside:

He pointed with his stick at a tree with a reddish trunk and a low crown.
"What's that tree?"
I didn't know.
"What's growing on that bush?"
I didn't know this either.

And so forth, with the names of birds, where they fly away to, even —astoundingly, yet credibly—on which side the sun rises.

What seems important is not the old man's perception that "a feeling for nature" is essential to a writer, but the truth that the boy has been led somehow to neglect not merely the natural world, but the very physical world itself, in which his own body must live. It is fitting and deeply traditional that in order to encounter this truth the boy must head down toward the docks, the Moldavanka district where the Jewish gangsters like Benya Krik rule: that is, toward the earth-shaking, massive, threatening and challenging domain of Poseidon, Odysseus's opponent.

Something I like in the story is that there is enough glory to go around for everyone: Nemanov at General Motors, Gabrilowitsch playing a recital before the Czar, the young writer deciding to climb trees. The scale of the ocean, and its message of possibility—any pitfall or wonder imaginable is in it somewhere—seems to encourage the idea of measuring human life, with its names and desires, against the preposterously enormous backdrop. That is why the woman in "Eros Turannos" appears against that heroic back-drop. Such characters prove worthy of salt water.

It is ridiculous, but Izzy Ash's venture into allegory or Danny Pingitore's venture into Hollywood, toward fame, the whole Long Branch pantheon of Jeff Chandler, Barry Green, Vito Genovese, Norman Mailer, seems in my imagination also related to the over-whelming size and perpetual movement of the ocean. It is so big and changing and unchanging, its various noises are so evocative and musical, it suggests so much of heroic risk or gaudy pleasure, that the imagination is nudged by its presence in extravagant directions.

Everybody carries their own rulers and scales with them. When I arrived in California, I had never seen land elevated beyond the hundred feet or so of Atlantic Highlands, or the rolling hills near the Delaware. The Sierras astonished me. The clarity and immensity of the air and rock, the extent and nakedness of the light were things I had not imagined. Kodak dyes fail to indicate the penetration and subtlety of the colors. In a sense, I was like the archetypal provincial gaping at the towers of Manhattan. But, for the scope and grandeur of size—though here the first big impression is of how much can be seen, while at home it is how much may remain hidden, out and below—I did have a standard to bring. And there is an ocean here, to help me feel at home and to remind me that I come from someplace.

—Berkeley, 1982

T. S. Eliot: A Memoir

Elegant, unassuming, firm, energized by the freedom of the amateur and forged by the knowledge of the artist, with a manner so fine and fluent that it seemed to rise up into separate atoms that irradiated to create a whole world, where large numbers of people shared "the mind of Europe" and mused about such questions as "What is a Classic" or "What is Minor Poetry," a world strikingly unlike New Brunswick, New Jersey, where I went to college, the essays of T. S. Eliot, through that world-conjuring perfume of their manner more than through their content, had hypnotic authority for me in those days.

"The Waste Land" was a great poem, and "Four Quartets" a great mystery. "The Love Song of J. Alfred Prufrock" was near the center of my idea of poetry, but though I read Eliot's poems with great excitement, I don't think I read any of them over and over again quite the way I read certain poems of Yeats. (My roommate and I had typed up "Sailing to Byzantium" and tacked it over the kitchen table like a poster.) It was the essays and—I am ashamed to say—their superbly understated confidence and snooty, self-effacing brilliance that got under my skin. Rutgers was a nervous, stagnant underfed little state university, so intent on aping the sham gentility of Princeton that it could barely communicate to us hicks and diamonds-in-the-rough that there amid the Hungarian gas stations and tarpaper bars we were being offered a superlative literary education. My teachers included Francis Fergusson, author of *The Idea of a Theatre,* a great and good man, and Paul Fussell, my Freshman Composition instructor, who later wrote brilliantly about the Great War, and about snobbery. Neither of these teachers fits in the least the stereotype of the Eliot-worshiping New Critic of the 1950s, but both added their authority to that musing, cultivated, quietly audacious voice.

Because I understood the actual meanings of the essays so imperfectly, distracted as I was by their manners, I blundered around quite a lot trying to write poems with objective correlatives and the mind of Europe in them. This was no fault of Eliot the writer; I had apprenticed myself unconsciously to a persona. Because I knew Spanish but not French, I wrote one poem which quoted *"¿Qué se fizo el Rey don Juan?,"* rhyming the king's name with "gone," and another quoting the Romance in which a penitent and adulterous king, being eaten in his tomb by a dragon, sings:

"Ya me come, ya me come,
por do más pecado había."

That is, "Now he is eating me there where I have sinned the most." For me, this grotesque and flamboyant royal penance could only have represented strong color, and maybe a little wishful thinking about the transgressions that preceded it. From composing allusive rubbish of this kind I felt delivered by various works, of which I definitely remember three: Allen Ginsberg's *Howl,* Dudley Fitts's *Poems From the Greek Anthology,* and Alan Dugan's *Poems.*

I was fascinated by the brevity, clarity and freshness of the poems Fitts translated, on the spare pages of the New Directions paperback, each poem framed vertically by title and author's name in all caps, many of the poems only five or six lines long. The range of emotion in these poems—a quick burst of love or rage, a passionate longing, contempt, a joke, a plea, a horny groan or irritated bark turned into a move quick and graceful as some gesture in basketball—was like a reproach to my oblique, cramped "mind of Europe" phase. Reading Ginsberg was like discovering you were born knowing how to play an instrument. The rhythm of the lines and fountainlike phrases was attractive, but even more exciting was the rhythm of invention, coming out of a rebellious yet familial turning-back upon literature, religion and the newspaper their own lushness and spaciousness and variety. And I found something of both the Greek epigram's blade and Ginsberg's ebullience in Dugan's elegant, mocking, weepy meditations on farts and rotten teeth, religion and history. The most important thing about these books, in a way, was that they had not been assigned in school, were not required reading.

Of course, it was the poems of Eliot and Pound that enabled me to read these books with some understanding. The rhythms and idiom Fitts used to translate Meleagros's

A LOVER'S CURSE

This thing I pray, dearest Night, Mother of the gods:
This thing only I pray, holy propitious Night:

If another man lies with her now: if another
Close-clasped beneath her cloak, is touching her—
Heliodora, Heliodora, the sweet despair of sleep—

Then let the light go out!
       Let his
Heavy eyes fail him!
       Let him fall asleep
Locked in her arms, a second Endymion!

were clear to me because I had read poems from *Ripostes* and *Lustra,* where the same cadences and sculpted simplicity worked in a similar way.

Even the note of mingled skepticism, knowing self-pity, vulgar laughter and triple-soured Byronic wit, that so delighted me in Dugan's work:

THIS MORNING HERE

This is this morning: all
the evils and glories of last night
are gone except for their
effects: the great world wars
I and II, the great marriage
of Edward the VII or VIII
to Wallis Warfield Simpson and
the rockets numbered like the Popes
have incandesced in flight
or broken on the moon: now
the new day with its famous
beauties to be seized at once
has started and the clerks

have swept the sidewalks
to the curb, the glass doors
are open, and the first
customers walk up and down,

was the more apprehensible because I had read:

I shall not want Honour in Heaven
   For I shall meet Sir Philip Sidney
And have talk with Coriolanus
   And other heroes of that kidney.

I shall not want Capital in Heaven
   For I shall meet Sir Alfred Mond.
We two shall lie together, lapt
   In a five per cent. Exchequer Bond.

I shall not want Society in Heaven,
   Lucretia Borgia shall be my Bride;
Her anecdotes will be more amusing
   Than Pipit's experience could provide.

In fact, even this lesser poem of Eliot's seems to embody what I thrilled to most in poetry: the clangorous, barely-harmonized bringing together of the sacred and profane. The modern poetry that means the most to us seems to create essential energy from that fusion or disparity. Ginsberg, for example, could hardly address Moloch, or evoke the gyzym of consciousness in Turkish baths and Mohammedan angels on tenement roofs above the El, without it.

Eliot is above all the pre-eminent poet of this clash or yoking, as a multitude of familiar passages recall:

At the violet hour, when the eyes and back
Turn upward from the desk, when the human engine waits
Like a taxi throbbing waiting,
I Tiresias, though blind, throbbing between two lives,
Old man with wrinkled female breasts, can see
At the violet hour, the evening hour that strives
Homeward, and brings the sailor home from the sea,
The typist home at teatime.

The two lives here are not simply the lives of two sexes, but the inward and outward life, the life of experience and of some imagined ideal. Because he identified and penetrated this dualism in the rhythms and noises and smells and surfaces of modern life, without simplifying what he saw into false ideas of squalor or perfection, Eliot remains entirely essential for us. He is not merely whatever we mean by "great poet," but precisely what Pound means by "an inventor." For this, Eliot's readers forgive him his mean side, his religio-authoritarian claptrap, the plushy grandiosity of "Ash Wednesday," the tetrameter anti-Semitism, the genteel trivialities of the late plays.

It appears to me that while in a sort of social way, at the level of will, I spent my sophomore year courting what I imagined was the spirit of *On Poetry and Poets,* on a deeper level I was absorbing the moral drama of "Prufrock" and "The Waste Land" and "Four Quartets," the complex and unyielding collision between the imagination of Paradise on one side and the experience of modern life on the other. Even the pathetic macaronic verses about King Juan, and King Rodrigo's last song to his confessor, must have been affected by Eliot's imagination of this collision.

One personal result of all this, for me, is a kind of pitying mistrust toward all literary criticism: it seems to me that as a form, writing about poetry, especially, is doomed to be misunderstood and garbled. And fickle as taste in art may be, I think taste in criticism is a hundred times more fickle. If critical work is elevated by fashion, it is absolutely certain eventually to be thrown down. True poetry, on the other hand, is never really misunderstood or discarded, because its basis is in pleasure. Explanations and theories are misunderstood; pleasures are either had, or not.

This is a personal conviction, and may stem partly from the experience I have tried to describe, of feeling captured by Eliot's prose while I was more deeply being educated into poetry by his poems. It is as if criticism belongs to the marketplace, or to the imagination, and only art can comprehend both at once:

> We have lingered in the chambers of the sea
> By sea-girls wreathed with seaweed red and brown
> Till human voices wake us, and we drown.

It is only poetry itself that can attend to both human voices and the chambers of the sea. It is Eliot more than anyone else who has awakened us, in our modern world, to the extremes in art of such double attention.

Poland I: Form and Freedom

This is a personal essay. I'd like to explore the ideas of form, freedom and control by leading up to a particular time when I was brought to consider a poem of mine in a cultural setting just a little different from my accustomed one. Some of the material will be autobiographical, and I'll risk some generalities by way of introduction.

I think that I have always assumed unconsciously that people want poetry. Their desire may take astoundingly debased forms, or even be totally frustrated and quiescent, but—perhaps through complacency or egocentrism—I have never truly doubted the idea, an idea which I think I first formulated for myself when I read William Morris's moving, perhaps ludicrous words about rioters in the streets outside his house:

> As I sit at my work at home, which is at Hammersmith, close to the river, I often hear some of that ruffianism go past the window of which a good deal has been said in the papers of late, and has been said before at recurring periods. As I hear the yells and shrieks and all the degradation cast on the glorious tongue of Shakespeare and Milton, as I see the brutal reckless faces and figures go past me, it rouses the recklessness and brutality in me also, and fierce wrath takes possession of me, till I remember, as I hope I mostly do, that it was my good luck only of being born respectable and rich, that has put me on this side of the window among delightful books and lovely works of art, and not on the other side, in the empty street, the drink-steeped liquor shops, the foul and degraded lodgings. I know by my own feelings and desires what these men want, what would have saved them from this lowest depth of savagery: employment which would foster their self-respect and win the praise and sympathy of their fellows, and dwellings which they could come to with pleasure, surroundings which would soothe and elevate

them; reasonable labour, reasonable rest. There is only one thing that can give them this—art.

Engels said about Morris that his thinking was alright for a half-hour or so after he had a thing explained to him. But in this case, I think he is following his intuition to a peculiar truth.

I don't know if there are, in fact, cultures in which the appetite for poetry does not appear. If an expert told me that there were such cultures, I probably would doubt his evidence, out of the provincial need to believe that one's particular pursuit is universal, or if not universal, then universally craved. And yet the nature of poetry is so unknown, so little theory of it satisfies as final truth, that if another expert on cultures asserted that in every culture on earth there is an appetite for poetry, there would be a temptation to doubt him, too.

The distinction between the art and the craving for the art is highly artificial. (I think it occurs to me because of Isak Dinesen's account of inventing the first rhymed phrases in a language, to the delight of the language's native speakers, who urged her to "talk like rain"; this story seems, I confess, like a constructed fable or a misapprehension.) But just the same, the artificial distinction tells me something about my own feelings toward the art of poetry: the most deep and mysterious quality of that art, for me, is the bodily role of the sounds of language; and the mystery inheres less in the actual rhythms themselves (which can sometimes, on a crude level, be analyzed in part) than in our desire for them. The desire for the essential, physical aspect of poetry, its arrangement of sounds, seems to be a desire both for art and for the bodily. As such, my experience of the appetite for poetry is protean, mysterious (I wish I could vary that term) and quite resistant to even rough analysis. This is not a bardic or sentimental assertion; that is, the appetite for poetry has the same mystery as all of the cravings that could be called, old-fashionedly, the human appetites; the desire for cuisine, beyond nutrition; for eroticism, beyond sexuality.

These appetites, perhaps by definition, both challenge and invite control. It can be argued—though I reject this idea—that they are subtle forms of control. That is, by various theories the desire for cuisine, eroticism or poetry might be understood as a social harnessing (or exploitation, or perversion, depending upon the theory) of my natural appetite for food, sex or information. But the appetite for art also seems to free me from the social facts about me, that I was born in 1940 to Milford and Sylvia Pinsky, in Long Branch, New Jersey, and so forth. If social facts control us, control is (it is banal to say) what appetite pushes against.

Of course, appetites can be manipulated for control. And my ideas about what is delicious, poetic or erotic seem to be largely, some would say entirely, learned and cultural: study of some kind lies behind the spontaneity of a line of Stevens's pentameter, a new white dress or the dash of Worcestershire sauce. Something in me persists in thinking of such cultural pleasures as modes of freedom, rather than modes of repression or control. That something seems so crucial to me that I am shy to give it any of its possible names from the terms of political or intellectual-historical thought.

I am claiming that my idea of learned culture in general, and the rhythms of English poetry in particular, as modes of freedom, comes from inside me. I feel convinced that it is not merely or simply an ideology assimilated by the upward-striving, English-speaking descendant of ambitious steerage immigrants from Eastern Europe. Though I know what is meant by "control" in a work of art, and respect that idea, my main response to the idea of control is that it is something external, from which the artist profits by resisting it. Control is not the same as form.

I'll try to explain that conviction in personal terms. My memories of my early childhood, in a small seashore town in New Jersey, are happy. That happiness was sort of misted over, nearly forgotten, for years, because my adolescence was somewhat miserable, in familiar ways that I'd like to reexamine. I did very badly in school from about the seventh grade on. A couple of times I was "kicked out" for cutting classes, insubordination, failure to comply with rules or instructions, etc.

In fact, I always tried to be a pleasant and amusing companion to the students and teachers at school, and while in school I tried my best to do what would get one by, within the limits of my absent-minded, unsystematically anarchic nature. (I remember being particularly good at Plane Geometry, at sketching, and at translation from Latin to English, for instance, though I could never do better than a "D" in Latin overall.)

Why couldn't I get by more easily, then? Ultimately, I don't know. But in practice, my teachers were offended because all of my energy and ingenuity was invested in perfecting techniques for giving as little as possible to the official, public work of the school. I would be happy to do my best, in a sociable way, to discuss a character in *Julius Caesar,* when called on—why be rude? But I was bound by some unconscious code of behavior not to read *Julius Caesar*—as much as I might have liked to read it under other circumstances—precisely because I had been "assigned," that is, bound, to read it. Somehow, to ignore tests, homework, every mildest form of coercion, or contradiction of my will, had become a point of honor.

I hope that I am not boasting about this; something was wrong with me. (Though to tell the truth, the school was no better than it ought to be, either.) Like the authorities, I thought of my iron recalcitrance as "laziness" and "rebellion," though in fact it demanded great energy, and was in essence anarchic and friendly rather than rebellious; far from wanting to overturn or even to defy authority, I was miserably eager to please it, any way I could, short of doing what it told me to do. Why I couldn't do that, I don't feel sure.

When I might have been making my family and myself happy by doing a little (*even* a little) assigned reading, or memorizing a conjugation, I followed instead my version of what must be a standard pattern. That is, I did a thing of my own. In my case, this involved music: trying to imitate Lester Young and Stan Getz on the saxophone; working out improvisations and tunes on the keyboard; arranging bookings for the band at high school dances, bars, Elks' Clubs, weddings; doodling endless logos for the band, or heads of musicians; daydreaming about glory as a musician.

The point of this far from unique memoir may be clear already: my noodling and doodling with music expressed my craving for freedom. And in my bones I know that it was also a craving for art. In "Lester Leaps In" or Charlie Parker's choruses on "Just Friends" I found a haughty perfection and playfulness. This music made a whole inherited culture seem the instrument upon which one might play, rather than the other way around. The music of Young and Parker exploited certain historical circumstances—economics, Western instruments, this, that and the other—for personal expres-

sion, through the medium of an elegant form. Without having more
than a minimal aptitude for music, I found in it a repository for
the Romance of art, a way to prove and maintain my freedom from
the coercion of circumstance. Music, or perhaps the idea of music,
slaked and so preserved my appetite for freedom. Though I didn't
(of course) think of it this way, music was form, and it was my ally
against control. I think that this must be a common, perhaps typical
phenomenon in middle-class American teen-age life.

In contrast, when my maternal grandfather, Morris, was about
thirteen, he left his home town of Grodno, then in Poland and now
in the Soviet Union, and made his way slowly to the German port
of Lübeck, from which he sailed for America, landing in Galveston,
Texas. (Apparently my father's paternal grandfather, about whom
I know less, also came from Grodno, presumably leaving some years
earlier; his son was my Grandpa Dave, the gangster and prize-
fighter.) At eleven or twelve, Grandpa Morris had been arrested for
handing out political pamphlets of an inflammatory kind, then
managed to get released by pretending that he could not understand
Russian, the language of the pamphlet. He was a Jew, and he hoped
to find abundance and freedom in America, where he has subse-
quently traveled extensively (he is still alive) by car, train and
motorcycle. When my mother was born, I believe he was a partner
in a motorcycle repair business in Little Rock, Arkansas. Though
he never became quite prosperous by American standards, he raised
his family in what must be considered abundance and freedom,
compared to what he left behind. (Needless to say, had he remained
in Grodno, it is very likely that he and his seed would have been
brutally and thoroughly wiped out.) For him, American culture was
in a practical way an instrument of freedom.

At this point I'd like to recount the instance of cultural contrast
and overlap I referred to at the outset. About seventy-five or eighty
years after my grandfather left Grodno, I was sent by the cultural
branch of the American Department of State on a tour of several
Eastern European countries, to read from my poems and to talk
informally with writers, scholars and students about American po-
etry. This tour began with a week in Poland, and by blind luck the
time was within six months of the amazing events of August, 1980,
when shipyard workers in Gdansk challenged the system, igniting

a genuine proletarian revolution. Many of the writers and intellectuals I met were direct beneficiaries of this revolution, in the form of increased freedom of basic sorts: freedom to travel, to publish one's work, to form organizations openly, to speak, to sign one's real name to a piece of writing.

A bit more background is necessary. The week I arrived, the second week in March, was the anniversary of the risings of 1968, when demonstrators had been clubbed by police. Now, in 1981, exultant students of the University of Warsaw, bearing red-and-white "Solidarnosc" emblems, demonstrated by the thousands. These demonstrations took place on my second day in Warsaw. That same day, on the other side of the park (having been leveled by bombs, Warsaw is full of green space) a smaller counter-demonstration took place, led by an actor of sorts; this counter-demonstration, estimated variously as being of a few hundred people up to a thousand, was anti-Semitic in nature.

The actor and his group were taking a line based on history: if Poles were going to commemorate past brutalities, they said, then the late forties and early fifties must be remembered. Though this group's logic and motives were equally contemptible, they were referring to certain historical facts. In the Stalinist Politburo of the Polish Party were a number of people who had sat out the war in Moscow, returning after the war to take office under the aegis of Russian power. Some of these people (for still other historical reasons) were Jewish, and among those was the head of the Internal Police. During his administration, many people were tortured. The actor and his friends described those tortures as Zionist abuses, and their counter-demonstrations of March, 1981, represented a semi-official or covertly official attempt by elements within the government to deflect or divide Solidarity. They called for a purging of Zionist influences from Solidarity. This attempt at dividing and confusing dissent by waving the banner of anti-Semitism appears to have failed, perhaps because, as many journalists have pointed out, the last governmental anti-Semitic campaign, in 1968 (again, more history), left Poland on the verge of becoming a country with anti-Semitism but no Jews.

As for me, my first responses to all of this history, so much of it nasty and appalling, were those of a kind of hick; it struck me that as an American I had possibly (tritely enough) underestimated history—underestimated the extent to which vile forces and dark, bitter roles might be in people's blood: even, in a sense, in my blood. That is, the conditions of birth and ancestry mattered more than I was used to. I felt childish, or perhaps childlike is the word. The torture that had most concerned me in my lifetime was the torture I knew had been learned as a technique in certain American agencies, by students who returned to their homes as military and police officials in such countries as Chile, Argentina, El Salvador, Nicaragua, Iran; my imagination of my country had been affected in certain widespread, ineluctable ways by the prolonged attempt to force American will on Southeast Asia by means of decimation. My instinct for freedom, in a way, had drawn an intuitive, ahistorical, permanent line leftward from jazz to liberation. Now, I was in a country where the Ku Klux Klan cited history, and history that encompassed me, by blood.

In Poland, I was eager to take in everything I could, and in relation to the counter-demonstrations and to much else, I concentrated hard on being a movie-camera. I concentrated so hard on recording mentally as much as I could of what I saw that what I actually thought was often embarrassingly petty or trivial. In relation to the anti-Semitic demonstrations, what I thought included the fact that I had used the phrase "anti-Semitic" in one of my poems —but with a lot of spin on the phrase, so to speak. The poem was one of the ones that had been translated into Polish; I hoped that the anti-Semitic demonstrations, and the background that they embodied, would not distort the poem when it was read aloud at the Writer's Union the next day.

Perhaps this farcically self-centered viewpoint, reminiscent of the Jack Benny character in *To Be or Not to Be,* is related to the feeling that one might be willing to read *Julius Caesar,* but not as part of a group required to read it by a certain day. Anyway, the fact of the poem, of American poetry in general, its rhythms and its language, made me feel free from Poland and—as much as I liked and admired the Poles—from its stinking history.

The poem is called "Poem About People":

The jaunty, crop-haired graying
Women in grocery stores,

Their clothes boyish and neat,
New mittens or clean sneakers,

Clean hands, hips not bad still,
Buying ice cream, steaks, soda,
Fresh melons and soap—or the big
Balding young men in work shoes

And green work pants, beer belly
And white T-shirt, the porky walk
Back to the truck, polite; possible
To feel briefly like Jesus,

A gust of diffuse tenderness
Crossing the dark spaces
To where the dry self burrows
Or nests, something that stirs,

Watching the kinds of people
On the street for a while—
But how love falters and flags
When anyone's difficult eyes come

Into focus, terrible gaze of a unique
Soul, its need unlovable: my friend
In his divorced schoolteacher
Apartment, his own unsuspected

Paintings hung everywhere,
Which his wife kept in a closet—
Not, he says, that she wasn't
Perfectly right; or me, mis-hearing

My rock radio sing my self-pity:
"The Angels Wished Him Dead"—all
The hideous, sudden stare of self,
Soul showing through like the lizard

Ancestry showing in the frontal gaze
Of a robin busy on the lawn.

In the movies, when the sensitive
Young Jewish soldier nearly drowns

Trying to rescue the thrashing
Anti-semitic bully, swimming across
The river raked by nazi fire,
The awful part is the part truth:

Hate my whole kind, but me,
Love me for myself. The weather
Changes in the black of night,
And the dream-wind, bowling across

The sopping open spaces
Of roads, golf-courses, parking lots,
Flails a commotion
In the dripping treetops,

Tries a half-rotten shingle
Or a down-hung branch, and we
All dream it, the dark wind crossing
The wide spaces between us.

I give the poem here, not in order to talk about it in itself, but in order to deal with the way it incidentally provided the occasion for an instance of cultural parallax.

A young poet who was interpreting for me was about to read the Polish version of "Poem About People" (not his own translation) to a group of older writers. I felt suddenly that I wanted to say a word or two of gloss; so I said that in the few days I had been in Poland I had become aware that in Poland the expression "anti-Semitism" referred to a potentially powerful political motive force, capable of moving large numbers of people. For an American of my generation, I said, anti-Semitism could be treated as primarily a matter of manners, if one so chose, rather than politics. In American, everyone was a dirty something-or-the-other, and because it was not already a powerful symbol within national life, "anti-Semitism" might even be used in a poem partly as a symbol. It might even be used partly as a comic manifestation—one might choose to treat anti-Semitism in America as a kind of bad manners, like someone chewing with his mouth open, letting gravy trickle down his chin and onto his vest. It might offend, even hurt someone's feelings, but its political impact was negligible.

I think that this was partly half-conscious bravado, a calculated counterattack. If being American made me an innocent hick or a child in relation to the anti-Semitism of Poland, then being American also entitled me to something resembling aristocratic disdain toward it. If my grandfather left the country by easing himself out from under Polish history, I was coming to it from outside and above, by TWA and embassy Plymouth. In part, I suppose, I was an American high-school wise guy, trying to needle a whole culture as if it were a group of grown-ups, some of whom had offended me. I declined to be anyone's even potential victim. The film *The Young Lions,* in which Montgomery Clift, sensitive young Jewish soldier, rescues the bullies and so forth, was an absurd, rather appealing bit of *my* culture; the Polish actor and his sleazy, creepy counter-demonstration were not.

The writers chuckled at the table-manners trope, and the meeting with them was congenial and lively. But afterward, the young poet who had read the Polish versions said, "They liked that poem very much, you know . . . but about the anti-Semitism, what you said when they laughed—I think that none of them believed you."

Well, yes. In a sense, they were right to doubt my explanation, which was perhaps too rosy and patriotic. Thinking about the poem, I was glad that it was itself, for good or ill, and not its gloss or its explanation. One should confide in the poems, and abjure gloss and explanation altogether, maybe . . . but all the same I was annoyed with them, a little: annoyed on my country's behalf, because even if I had exaggerated its generosity, perhaps, or its pure freedom from bloody European mania, in some other sense I was right: give or take a few country clubs with terrible food, or fraternity houses with boring company, my grandfather had done very handsomely by me; and even if his descendants had survived in Poland, they couldn't have begun to make even a somewhat disingenuous speech about their freedom from other people's ideas about what "Jew" would mean for them, to them, about them.

But the annoyance on my country's behalf was superficial compared with the deeper annoyance that they were telling me who I was—that I was perhaps a more historically determined creature than I might conceivably choose to be. From that perspective, the young poet who had read out the translations may have been intuitively siding with me when he said "they" didn't believe me. When *Annie Hall* was shown at the American Embassy, one Polish scriptwriter present had enormous difficulty believing that Woody Allen was Jewish (let alone understanding why the Americans present found the idea of a non-Jewish Woody Allen funny): How could Allen feel free to make the jokes he makes in *Annie Hall,* how could he be bold enough to conceive its form?

Perhaps it is the exhilaration of any form to push against some confining expectation. In the America of the 1950s, Frank O'Hara (e.g., in "A Step Away from Them") and Allen Ginsberg ("America, I'm putting my queer shoulder to the wheel") wrote poems of great formal invention and boldness; part of the formal exhilaration of those poems certainly is a sense as of the artist being himself. The control of sexual tastes and behavior implied by the mores of the Eisenhower years—Ike and Mamie listening to Fred Waring and the Pennsylvanians—was something for O'Hara and Ginsberg to push against. The forms they attain (unpredictable, swift and exuberant or Whitmanian, comic and melancholy) do not express or transcend or defend "homosexuality." Rather, they seem to say, "it is *my* 'homosexuality,' not anyone else's, or anyone else's idea of it." They at most express "homosexuality" as another form of freedom —one person's freedom, perhaps—rather than as a category; this is analogous to the sense that one's own body is a form of freedom because it is in detail different from every other body.

I like to think that it was thrilling for the young, ambitious nobleman Philip Sidney, writing the sonnets that he circulated among an elite of family and friends, to feel that his imitations of Petrarch were something new, and English: English in a way that was his way, as his body was his. Artificial and contrived as *Astrophil and Stella* may be in one way, he did in another way look into his heart to write it, as he says he did. To be sweepingly optimistic about such questions, perhaps every historical circumstance, every limitation of politics or inherited identity, is something to push against, a possible control. Perhaps form, in its truest manifestations, must be an appetite, an appetite for being autonomous and oneself, more bold and naked than any external preconception of oneself. A poem may be the least confused, most free thing one says (or hears) because it is the most deliberately physical, and so the most naked. Form expresses the craving to be free of imposed, controlling abstractions. It is a made, bodily abstraction to challenge the abstractions of circumstance.

In Poland, amid a time of surprising, inspiring new freedom for the country, I was invited by chance to think of myself as more historically determined than I had before. Striving to think of that as a writer's problem, a formal problem, I felt a renewed sympathy for every sullen student doodling, on the overflowing margins of some grubby notebook, a name or face.

Poland II: Solidarity Days

The visiting American poet, in his capacity as an item of cultural exchange, is put up in Poznan's official tourist hotel. In the lobby, members of the semi-legal Rural Solidarity are meeting in small workshop-sized groups. Many of them look the way farmers are expected to look: big, determined-looking men of various ages in bulky dress-up clothes, and wearing green "Solidarnosc" pins in their lapels. A fair number of women also attend. There is something odd and unfamiliar about the intensity of these committee meetings; there don't seem to be any glazed expressions, smirks, finger-twiddling. Nobody is staring at the ceiling or his shoes. People are talking with a concentration that confirms a sense one gets from the literary people in Warsaw and Krakow, or from the way people date time as "before August" or "since August": these beefy, passionately debating farmers are sharing the heady atmosphere of successful revolt and new freedom. However brief it may turn out to be, and however complex its causes and meanings, this new freedom is also shared by the poets, translators, editors and screenwriters I meet. And it began, amazingly enough, with a proletarian uprising in the shipyards of Gdansk, in August.

At one end of the hotel lobby, a stocky farmer was addressing a tall one with furious energy and operatic gestures. I asked the poet I was with if he might eavesdrop and interpret a bit.

"The smaller guy is talking about the rights to union membership of beekeepers and mushroom growers, about how they mustn't be excluded just because they have fewer than the minimum number of hectacres." His smile was amused, but respectful rather than condescending toward the fervor of democratic debate this issue aroused.

At first, the legitimate passion centering on such matters seems to make cultural exchange ludicrous. Can recent literary developments in New York or California possibly be important to Poles these days? In the midst of the current intense hopes and fears, against the background of economic stress, I feel like a fairly ignorant, comic tourist, not only in Poland but in a remarkable historical moment. (At Solidarnosc's rickety headquarters in Warsaw, there's a desk where one can buy Solidarnosc T-shirts and souvenirs.) Yet even in the euphoric, anxious, charged atmosphere of renewal, shortages, food lines and reinstated non-persons, Poles turn out to have a surprising interest in writing and in what might seem the peripheral or exotic subject of contemporary American poetry.

Strange as it seems, one meets people who quote Frost, Williams and Stevens in English from memory. Stranger still, they want up-to-date information about recent American poetry: What do I think of John Ashbery's new book? James Merrill's? Why does e. e. cummings seem to be out of style in America? Which have the greater influence among young poets, one student wants to know, the Beats or the Confessionals? Why do I think Elizabeth Bishop is so important? Partly, this eagerness seems to express the way a feeling of autonomy and shared purpose can make people alert to everything around them. (As a dim analogy, I try comparing it to the way in which American students, on strike in the spring of 1970, became interested in an encyclopedic range of subjects; similarly, I try to compare, also dimly, the energy and focus of those farmers to the intensity of American civil-rights workers during the fleeting time when the expression "the Movement" carried conviction.)

But the considerable excitement inspired here by the words "American" and "poetry" has other roots as well. Startlingly, a student explains her view that the poet must be a rebel against the constraints of society: How, then, can an American poet possibly write? A peculiar moment; rather than talk about our domestic injustices, or our relations with Latin America or South Africa, still less about the alienation that American artists have been said to carry around like a union card, it seems best to present examples, beginning with the mingled exasperation and love of William Carlos Williams's "The pure products of America go crazy."

I feel at times like a purely innocent American product myself, trying to imagine the feelings of the intellectuals and writers I meet. Many of them were "prohibit" before August—removed from jobs, or from influence, prevented from above-ground publication or limited to pseudonyms. For a magazine editor to have published translations of Richard Crashaw and Thomas Traherne executed by an "unreliable" person, even though the translations were attributed to a pseudonym, was an act of courage. And now, people seem as outspoken as in Berkeley or New York. A young writer pauses on a street in Warsaw, to gesture at a wall: "Look at that, *political posters;* before August, unthinkable . . ." His tone is akin to the ineffable note of amusement, delighted surprise, wryness of an editor talking about relaxed censorship and new opportunities: with a little ironic lilt in his voice, he says, "And it's a present given to us by the workers." Increased freedom of expression and the reinstatement of banned teachers and writers appeared on the Solidarity bills of particulars along with such items as environmental protection. (A poisonous steel-mill stink hangs over Krakow, crumbling the ancient buildings that escaped the bombs of World War II.)

The sweeping idealism that keeps both freedom of expression and clean air on its list stands against the possibility of invasion. "Will they or won't they?" is a recurrent, more or less unavoidable topic at literary gatherings. With what I take to be an Eastern European habit of oblique reference whether it's necessary or not, the idea of Soviet invasion tends to be alluded to in ironic terms: "If our brothers drop in," "If company comes from the East," "If the Russian cultural exchange arrives" and so forth. The Polish writers I meet fall into an interesting conversational pattern on this topic. "Personally," many of them begin, "I am a pessimist." The speaker then goes on to list all of the reasons for an invasion *not* to take place: the Russians do not want to inherit the economic mess, the West is stronger than in 1968, the occupation would be too difficult, Afghanistan is distracting, the Western European Communists would abandon ship . . . the Pope . . . the Army . . .

I used the expression "if the worst happens" in a group, and an American who had been in the country for some time observed, "The worst has happened here so often." This seems to be the attitude of many Poles as they face, at the least, an excruciating war of nerves. Everyone has a memory of wartime death in the family. Everyone has to allot a few hours each day to waiting in line at shops whose shelves are mostly empty or decorated with meaningless items like tea boxes. (One of the most coveted black-market items is an English dictionary.) But among the kinds of people who go to poetry readings, anyway, there is an awesome feeling of hopefulness and determination. This infectious, bracing attitude has its complicated side for a visitor whose thinking is far more clear and expert on the subject of prosody than on that of politics. For instance, the pro-American feeling among the literary people here, and in fact everywhere I read my poems or lecture on this tour of Eastern Europe (Hungary, Romania, East Berlin), throws me a little off balance. No one seems to have heard of El Salvador, not even in East Berlin, the only place where *anyone* refers to the system, with a straight face, as "socialist." (The Polish writer Michael Szkolny, in an article on Solidarity in a recent *London Review of Books,* distinguishes true "socialism" from Soviet "state collectivism.")

I feel on safer ground in knowing where my sympathies lie. I will always associate Poland at this point in its history with Stanislaw Baranczak, the gifted young poet, critic and translator from English (of G. M. Hopkins among others). He is a kind of ex-non-person. Dissenting views in the seventies had placed him in the official cold. He was a non-person of such well-known, prolific talent and energy, however, that the strikers of August demanded—successfully —that he be reinstated in his university job.

When I arrived, Mr. Baranczak had been waiting a couple of years for an exit visa in order to accept a longstanding invitation to teach at Harvard. Semester after semester his visa was denied. In official eclipse, meanwhile, Mr. Baranczak continued to publish under various names. (Some of these were thin, perfunctory disguises, I am told by people who have followed his work in Polish.)

On the day I saw him, final word was promised on a new exit-visa application, for a new semester. It was a busy day for him. He interpreted and read his translations of the visiting American's poems at a morning meeting with the Writer's Union, went to lunch, was interviewed by an American journalist, interpreted again for a radio interview, then interpreted and read translations once more at an evening poetry reading. During the Writer's Union meeting, his wife, who had been waiting in line for word at the Passport Bureau, appeared with the news: no news, they will notify you tomorrow. Still miraculously calm, Mr. Baranczak interpreted at another interview after the reading, then excused himself—he had to return to the room where the reading had taken place. Why? He was chairing a meeting of students and teachers (much of the poetry audience simply remained in the room) related to the anniversary of the March, 1968, risings and police violence.

(It's a pleasure to report that two days later Mr. Baranczak received his visa. He is now living with his family in Cambridge, Massachusetts. I hope he can bear the pace there.)

The large nationwide demonstrations commemorating March, 1968 (roughly analogous to Kent State), when some of the seeds of the present renewal were sown, provided the occasion for the anti-Semitic counter-demonstrations that have received publicity in the West. There's a lot to be said about Polish anti-Semitism, but perhaps the most important practical point about these counter-demonstrations is that, unlike previous official attempts to use anti-Semitism as a means to weaken and divide dissent, these did not seem to work. "That card cannot be played again," said one Polish writer. A liberal Catholic editor told me, with the air of a man making an exquisite joke, that the demonstrators were "horrible bastards, Ku Klux Klan; but after all"—here he could barely contain himself—"what can you do, we are a free society now!"

Jokes like that one require a certain alertness to the ironic interweavings of memory and history in Poland. I have found Czeslaw Milosz's writing, especially his prose works, a useful guide to such matters. In particular, "Native Realm," Mr. Milosz's intellectual autobiography (subtitled "A Search for Self-Definition"), contains useful information about enduring Polish attitudes and responses. I'll close these notes with an example that may also illuminate the problem of anti-Semitism a little.

At a party attended by young translators and film people, one young man, an admirer of Thomas Pynchon, William Gaddis and Robert Coover, surprised me by being the only person I met in Poland who thought that Nobel Laureate Milosz was, flatly, "a bad poet." Mr. Milosz's very name was interdicted before the prize and the national wave of Renewal; now, the humanistic, anti-totalitarian poet has become a kind of national bard in people's minds, with long queues waiting to buy his poems, which sell out in large (albeit somewhat politically selected) editions. These lines were even longer than the lines for meat and butter.

The young translator's reasons for dissenting about Mr. Milosz were vague. Our conversation turned to anti-Semitism. He explained, variously and at length, how it was "justified," while at the pauses I kept responding that of course he meant to say "caused" or "motivated"—until I realized, with a weird sensation, that he meant "justified."

He seemed nice enough otherwise, though a little garrulous: a tall fellow, very American-sounding in speech, with a neatly trimmed beard, shoulder-length hair, a black velvet sports jacket and an open-throated shirt. His bland, humorless disquisition on the subject of anti-Semitism, his irritable rejection of Mr. Milosz, and his superb American English suddenly fit together, like the pieces of a puzzle, with one more bit of information: he had learned his English at various American schools in the foreign cities where his father had been posted as a diplomat.

"Diplomat" rang a bell. As other Poles present began saying—some shouting at him with a kind of pugnacious good will—he had swallowed certain Government propaganda, and the propaganda of "state collectivism" meshed neatly with the inherited attitudes of the Polish "diplomatic class." It is the "diplomatic class," or those who would like to think of themselves that way for snobbish reasons, whose brand of nationalism—dim-witted and anti-Semitic among other things—Mr. Milosz rejects scornfully in "Native Realm."

Mr. Milosz's disgust with the pseudo-aristocratic snobbery and intellectual barrenness of the right-wing inherited tradition was as offensive to one group as his rejection of the Soviet regime was to another. But the two groups overlapped in the person of the American-seeming young reader of Thomas Pynchon, with his neat beard and get-up. Toward the end of our conversation he told me, in the tone of one explaining something conclusively, that his family had lived in the same part of Poland since the fourteenth century. That and the official Soviet reenforcement of his anti-Semitism together signified more about his mind than his attractive, only slightly dated Western grooming. For a reader of "Native Realm," it was like looking at an interesting new coloration in a variety of creature first described in a great master's text.

Some Passages of Isaiah

I

The vision of Isaiah the son of Amoz, which he saw concerning Judah and Jerusalem in the days of Uzziah, Jotham, Ahaz and Hezekiah, kings of Judah.

Hear, O heavens, and give ear, O earth: for the Lord hath spoken, I have nourished and brought up children, and they have rebelled against me.

Isaiah 1:1–2

Thus begins the first and greatest of the Books of the Prophets: with visionary authority, royal names, proud genealogy, cosmic scope, and an indictment of the rebellious children of the Lord.

My grandfather Pinsky's disregard for the practice of Judaism as a religion was so calm and perfect that he never, to my knowledge, had any occasion to express his contempt for piety and rabbi-craft —except implicitly, by living his profane and glamorous life. He was a professional boxer and then a bootlegger, an arrogant young tough born to an immigrant laborer's family in the coarse, combative America of James Cagney movies. Maybe his own grandparents had sold vodka to Polish peasants. When I knew him, he owned the Broadway Tavern, a horseplayer's and downtown bar on the main street of Long Branch, the New Jersey Shore town where I grew up. Many of Long Branch's town officials, and all of its senior police force, had been Grandpa Dave's colleagues during the gangster days of Prohibition.

He had a Protestant wife, his third. Her name was Della Lawyer, and he lived with her for many years before they were married. At Christmas, his five children—my aunts and uncles, a confusing mix with different mothers and religions—came, some of them with their own children, to his neat brick house for dinner. He always had a ten-foot Christmas tree. He drove Packards, and when I was very small he introduced me to Jack Dempsey.

If you told Grandpa Dave that he was in any sense not Jewish, or not Jewish enough, he would laugh. If you suggested that he was ashamed of being Jewish, probably he would be ready to punch you in the face. I cannot think of him as "assimilated," still less as a "non-believer." Assimilation suggests protective resemblance to some secure cultural middle, not Grandpa Dave's aggressive ways out on the raffish, sometimes criminal, fringes. Belief is not the issue. Technically speaking, I would define him as an idolator.

His ways are described by the words of Isaiah 2, "they please themselves in the children of strangers," and "they worship the work of their own hands, that which their own fingers have made." His soul was given to the attractions of the world, the world of the senses, the world made by man. Isaiah 2 concludes, with magnificent curtness, "Cease ye from man, whose breath is in his nostrils: for wherein is he to be accounted of?" This is not mere asceticism, which is based on denial, but the transcendence of idolatry. Grandpa Dave stood for the immense beauty and power of idolatry, the adoration of all that can be made and enjoyed by the human body, with breath in its nostrils.

But we—my mother and father and we children—were Orthodox, because of my mother's family. That is, we were nominally Orthodox; we kept kosher, and belonged to the Orthodox synagogue, where I was taught to chant by rote the Hebrew sounds of my Haftorah, the portion from the Books of the Prophets to be read on the Sabbath of a boy's Bar Mitzvah. Mine was a special Haftorah for the conjunction of the Sabbath and the New Moon, Isaiah 66: the exalted, terrifying and punitive concluding chapter, though nobody told me it was Isaiah, or what the words meant.

Laboriously through the hot summer of my final preparation I chanted after the teacher's voice, phrase by phrase. *"Kay aumar adashem, hashawmayim keesee: es bawnehaw."* Thus, in my first encounter with great poetry, I was deaf and blind to it. My Hebrew vocabulary was too small to keep up with the original, and Hebrew School does not use the language of the King James translation, in which my Haftorah begins:

Thus saith the Lord, The Heaven is my throne, and the earth is my footstool: where is the house that ye build unto me? and where is the place of my rest?

For all those things hath mine hand made, and all those things have been, saith the Lord: but to this man will I look, even to him that is poor and of a contrite spirit, and trembleth at my word.

Isaiah 66:1–2

If I have made everything you see, says God in the syllables I studied, then where in the world of the senses could you contrive to build a place for Me? Architecture is futile. Humility, a spirit apt for contrition, and fearfulness will prevail.

Moreover, worship itself may fail. In fatigue and boredom, I was curious enough to look at the *en face* translation of the Hebrew into the stilted, Victorian English of the Jewish prayer book. In the King James, the next verse of my Haftorah reads:

He that killeth an ox is as if he slew a man; he that sacrificeth a lamb, as if he cut off a dog's neck; he that offereth an oblation, as if he offered swine's blood; he that burneth incense, as if he blessed an idol. Yea, they have chosen their own ways, and their soul delighteth in their abominations.

Isaiah 66:3

Autocratic; ardent and monolithic; specific and categorical: this is the voice of Spirit, speaking here in the burning cadences, the harsh monosyllables and rolling Latinate inventions of the English language. All forms of worship and ritual uninformed by itself, says that Spirit or voice, amount to idolatry. It is the uncompromising voice of spiritual authority. In Isaiah, that voice is so strong I could hear its powerful demand, though not its beauty, through the muffling translation and the rote learning. If Grandpa Dave represented the allure of the secular world, his adversary was not God —and certainly was not my mother's father, mild Grandpa Eisenberg—but that voice. As soon as possible, I turned away from it toward the larger world where I eventually heard it again—clearer, and more demanding than ever—in Milton, Blake and Whitman.

But first of all, it was the voice of Isaiah. And its indictment of failed or unacceptable worship unites the three authors (or compilations) identified by scholarship: First Isaiah, the aristocratic moralist-courtier of chapters 1–39; Second Isaiah, the dark, lyrical Exile poet of 40–55; and the post-Exilic Third Isaiah of my Haftorah. Wrong or misguided worship unites these three writings thematically, a driving force underlying the book's diverse materials—political, visionary, liturgical.

For instance, I was proud that my Haftorah was astronomically distinguished, by the conjunction of the Sabbath and the New Moon. And therefore, if I had known what the verse meant, and known that it was the penultimate verse of all Isaiah, I might have relished singing Third Isaiah's "And it shall come to pass, that from one new moon to another, and from one Sabbath to another, shall all flesh come to worship before me, saith the Lord."

But on the other hand I might have found an ironic indictment of what I was doing in the first chapter of the prophet. There, First Isaiah adumbrates the dog's neck, the swine's blood, the repellent idol of his successor, associating them with the special Sabbath in which I took a little pride of a personal kind:

> Bring no more vain oblations; incense is an abomination unto me; the new moons and Sabbaths, the calling of assemblies, I cannot away with, it is iniquity, even the solemn meeting.

> Your new moons and your appointed feasts my soul hateth; they are a trouble unto me; I am weary to bear them.

Isaiah 1:13–14

The hollowness, foppery or degeneracy of worship is no better here than the haughty daughters of Zion in Chapter 3, who "walk with stretched forth necks and wanton eyes, walking and mincing as they go, and making a tinkling with their feet," and whose chains, bracelets, mufflers, bonnets, leg ornaments, headbands, earrings, crisping pins, wimples, hoods, fine linen, stomachers, veils and tinkling ornaments the courtier-prophet catalogues and denounces, to be punished in commensurate detail with scabs, denuded private parts, baldness, burning rashes, and stinks.

Perhaps empty worship is even worse than those mere worldly vanities. But it also resembles them: I was taught to chant, without knowing the meaning of the words I chanted, a fierce denunciation of hollow worship. The new moons and appointed feasts and hollow oblations make God tired. His soul hates them. Singing the words of this denunciation without understanding them, I was committing a kind of idolatry, less attractive and more tiring—to me as well as to God—than the kind practiced by the daughters of Zion, or Grandpa Dave.

But there is something too obvious, and even heartless, about that inviting irony. It would be cruel to blame me, cruel to blame the old men who ran the small-town synagogue. They were immigrants without much money or knowledge of the world or education among them. Some had been in concentration camps. Doubtless, they were not very comfortable with Hebrew themselves. The language they felt at home in was Yiddish, and I could speak only English. The man these elders paid to teach me was kind, though sometimes impatient, and he was fighting against the worldly forces that had entered me—through the air, through our nostrils—two generations before: the tinkling ornaments, the work of human hands, "that which their fingers have made," the pleasures of the children of strangers, the veils and wimples, the secular incense and music of Saturday mornings outside, in a small town on the ocean. The Saturday morning service, in the yellow synagogue on Second Avenue in Long Branch, went from nine o'clock to some time after noon. Outside, the shadows of idols grew shorter in the sun. Italian girls in adorable Communion dresses came to St. Anthony's across the street, and went.

My teacher, two generations too late for an ardent communal piety and a generation too early for the intellectual savor of literature and ideas, could hardly avoid the blind rote performance I have called idolatrous, hateful to God in the very words I was trained to mouth. In Brooklyn, in a big vigorous traditional Jewish community, boys could—perhaps—learn the spirit demanded by Isaiah. Or in some affluent, enlightened place Jewish children of both sexes might be encouraged as part of their religious training to understand the meaning of sacred texts, in a literary way. In my community, where the old men and young boys conducted the Sabbaths, neither way was open. The old men had succeeded spectacularly in adjusting to American culture, in a secular way—the progeny of Long Branch's Jewish shopkeepers included, in my father's generation, Norman Mailer, M. H. Abrams, and even a movie star, along with doctors, lawyers, business people. But in a religious way, they could not seem to evade the indictment of the prophet.

The characteristic Jewish falling-away from the faith—a drifting toward the sweets of the world, so different from the tormented process described by James Joyce, or a Protestant "crisis of belief" —seems to me in a way to reflect this dogged, passionate, fumbling way of cleaving to the faith. In both movements, the cleaving and the drifting away, the essence is something deferred, not present, certainly not in the actual flesh. God's very name is only named, never uttered. Grandpa Dave and the "Moorish" synagogue of yellow sandstone (nowadays it houses a Puerto Rican Baptist church) occupy different spaces in the same void between practice and spirit. The Book of Isaiah is a great poem of that void, though it is also more.

II

Astoundingly, it is in the very nature of Isaiah's call to prophecy —an integral part of his first contract with God—that his prophecy will be spurned. Bad worship and idolatry are Isaiah's dramatic materials. The idea toward which these materials churn is the inception of God's kingdom on earth; but the poem's emotion and movement grow with overwhelming force from the idea that the very words we read have been destined to go unheeded until the promised end, and that our worship will be false.

The relevant passage is the autobiographical Chapter 6, which begins with a melding of the circumstantial and the marvelous:

> In the year that king Uzziah died I saw also the Lord sitting upon a throne, high and lifted up, and his train filled the temple.
>
> Above it stood the seraphims; each one had six wings; with twain he covered his face, and with twain he covered his feet, and with twain he did fly.
>
> And one cried unto another, and said, Holy, holy, holy, is the Lord of hosts: the whole earth is full of his glory.
>
> Isaiah 6:1–3

Isaiah's first response to this vision is terror: "Woe is me, for I am undone; because I am a man of unclean lips, and I dwell in the midst of a people of unclean lips: for mine eyes have seen the King, the

Lord of Hosts" (6:5). But a seraph places a live coal from the altar upon Isaiah's lips, purifying him of iniquity and sin, so that when the Lord asks "Whom shall I send" the prophet answers "Here am I; send me."

Between the circumstantial and the marvelous, in the actual temple with its altar, distraught and "unclean" at the sight of God, purified by an image of pain and muteness, the new prophet receives a strange charge:

> And he said, Go, and tell this people, Hear ye indeed, but understand not; and see ye indeed, but perceive not.
>
> Make the heart of this people fat, and make their ears heavy, and shut their eyes; lest they see with their eyes, and hear with their ears, and understand with their heart, and convert, and be healed.
>
> Isaiah 6:9–10

The verbs "hear," "understand not," "see" and "perceive not" are imperatives, the challenge or taunt of God, transmitted by the prophet, to his people. The Revised Standard renders the passage so as to make the imperatives even more clear:

> And he said, "Go, and say to this people:
>   'Hear and hear, but do not understand;
>   see and see, but do not perceive.'
>
> Make the heart of this people fat,
>   and their ears heavy,
>   and shut their eyes;
> lest they see with their eyes,
>   and hear with their ears,
> and understand with their hearts,
>   and turn and be healed."

This is supremely strange. The deafness and blindness are not an expectation, nor are they even described here as the strange punishments for past deafness and blindness that logic would make them. Strange retribution: but even stranger as the first charge for a prophet, at the beginning of his career. Isaiah's mission is to prophecy to people who must be made to feel, to see and to hear in the wrong way, to disregard his message. Heedlessness and bad worship are their destiny.

This bleak beginning can only be the phase of a process. Isaiah responds to the Lord by asking how long that phase must last:

> Then said I, Lord, how long? And he answered, Until the cities be wasted without inhabitant, and the houses without man, and the land be utterly desolate,

> And the Lord have removed men far away, and there be a great forsaking in the midst of the land.

> But yet in it shall be a tenth, and it shall return, and shall be eaten: as a teil tree, and as an oak, whose substance is in them, when they cast their leaves: so the holy seed shall be the substance thereof.
>
> Isaiah 6:11–13

In the massive, eschatological scale of this answer, invoking the immensity of time as a response to Isaiah's personal mission and fate, lies the difference between truth and prophecy, a difference of degree. The utter strangeness of the six-winged seraphim—dragon-flies, griffins, hovering and hiding their legs and faces—encloses in an image the inscrutable moral and historical journey to final things. These are the creatures that bring the searing, paradoxically enabling fire of conscience to the prophet's lips, within the actual walls of the familiar, doomed Temple.

The mighty scale of prophecy, contrasted by Isaiah with the legal exactions, the rituals, the hypocrisies, the political considerations, the vanities, of daily life, was invisible to me, the undiligent student of poor exiles. Only the sensual force of poetry could forge and convey the immensity of that vision; in this sense the prophet had to be a poet. But in Hebrew translation class we limped endlessly through Genesis, without applying our small abilities elsewhere. That eschatological scale, which in Isaiah extends both apocalyptic destruction and the salvation of New Jerusalem to the whole world ("Look unto me, and be ye saved, all the ends of the earth" [45:22]) explains and justifies the obdurate, negative terms of the prophet's charge. Isaiah gives his son the name "A-Remnant-Will-Return," recognizing the immense devastation that must precede the certain, promised end. Though a remnant will return, the final redemption will be universal, global.

The cosmic scope, in a literary way, counterbalances the local, even familial rhythms of indictment and promise, threats and praises. And in an historical way, it is conceivable that Isaiah's vision of "a great forsaking," decimation upon decimation, could offer the imagination a frame for the still-recent Nazi horrors in Europe, indelible but vague nightmare. (Could my attraction toward Grandpa Dave's violence be partly a reaction to those unsettling newsreel images of helplessness?) I don't mean the repulsive idea of a just punishment by Holocaust—an idea that also happens to clash with Isaiah's lucid, cosmic fatalism—but something more like a stretching of the imagination to enable it for the dimensions of actual knowledge. This is one definition of poetry.

Certainly, Isaiah offers something like a commensurate poetry of cataclysm:

> For wickedness burneth as the fire: it shall devour the briers and thorns, and shall kindle in the thickets of the forest, and they shall mount up like the lifting up of smoke.

> Through the wrath of the Lord of hosts is the land darkened, and the people shall be as the fuel of the fire: no man shall spare his brother.

> And he shall snatch on the right hand, and be hungry, and he shall eat on the left hand, and they shall not be satisfied: they shall eat every man the flesh of his own arm.

> > Isaiah 9:18–20

This vision underlies and vivifies the idea of the remnant that will return as a seed. It will return when the wolf lies down with the lamb and the lion eats straw like the ox. "Their children also shall be dashed to pieces before their eyes; their houses shall be spoiled and their wives ravished" (Isaiah 13:16). Chapters 24–27 have been nicknamed by scholarship "The Little Apocalypse." The apocalyptic action within the whole of Isaiah springs first of all from universal destruction: "Therefore hath the curse devoured the earth, and they that dwell therein are desolate: therefore the inhabitants of the earth are burned, and few men left" (24:6).

This destructive movement leads to two nearly opposed themes. First, God's will is punitive and urgent—"For behold, the Lord cometh out of his place to punish the inhabitants of the earth for their iniquity: the earth also shall disclose her blood, and shall no more cover her slain" (26:21). Second, God's will is ultimately impenetrable and mysterious: "For the Lord shall rise up as in Mount Perazim, he shall be wroth as in the valley of Gibeon, that he may do his work, his strange work, and bring to pass his act, his strange act" (28:21).

Again, only the conviction of poetry can suspend these two ideas, God's just retribution and God's impenetrable "strangeness," in a single action. The idolatrous makers, the smith and carpenter of graven images in Chapter 44, ought to recognize that worshipping the residue of firewood, their own handiwork, is sacrilege. But they have been blinded: "None considereth in his heart, neither is there knowledge or understanding to say, I have burned part of it in the fire; yea, also have I baked bread on the coals thereof; I have roasted flesh and eaten it: and shall I make the residue thereof an abomination? Shall I fall down to the stock of a tree?" (44:19). The reason for this folly echoes Isaiah's call to prophecy in Chapter 6: "They have not known nor understood: for he hath shut their eyes, that they cannot see; and their hearts, that they cannot understand" (44:18). At the promised end, the skies will open and pour down righteousness in as universal, sudden and "strange" a manner as this terrible blindness and deafness. God will blot out transgressions, and a remnant will return, in a redemption of horror and violence on the unthinkable level of the *eschaton,* the end of time. In the clearest of terms:

I form the light, and create darkness: I make peace and create evil:
I the Lord do all these things.

Isaiah 45:7

This God, who will create a new heaven and a new earth, so that the former will not be remembered, is the God of last things. He can hold the horrors of history and the abominations of idolatry, lip-service and hypocrisy in his transcendent gaze. It is prophetic poetry that makes Him possible, in all His apparent contradictions. The ultimate prophecy requires that it go unheard. The *eschaton,* the idea of the end of time, seems to require, for conviction, a temporal embodiment. (For some Christians, Isaiah is the Old Testament book that most clearly presages incarnation and Jesus Christ.) Apocalypse has its profound meaning in the physical realm of the body, not that of the Word. The Word is already eternal, the violent end of time will not transform it; the body, with breath in its nostrils, the inhabitant of time, will be transformed utterly.

God's glory, in Isaiah, is both unfathomable and also a physical glory. If this were not so, the ridicule of the idolatrous smith and carpenter, worshipping leftover firewood, would lose its force. This glory is embodied by the prophet in many ways—in terrifying visions, in acts of worship, in the Temple—but most continually in poetry, the physical art of poetry. In the sense that it is the art that pulls verbal abstraction into its bodily frame, poetry is the most insistently physical art.

Physical art is precisely what my synagogue lacked. Poor, beleaguered, displaced, deprived of architecture by history, deprived with one exception of the physical drama and elegance that depend upon possession of a place, and deprived even of mere, vulgar prosperity, the Jews of Long Branch could supply, in the place of a shining physical glory, only the passionate but colorless light of observance.

The one exception was cantorial singing. Its mournful beauty was indeed embodied, unforgettably, by cantors the congregation hired for the High Holy Days, though the goal was to find a permanent *chazen.* Sometimes a man would come to Long Branch for a few months, until a better position turned up, or he was let go for some defect of character or terrible habit. They sang like angels, and carried themselves with the neurotic pride of sickly bullfighters— or of the artists that they were. What they sang was a plaintive courtship between suffering and beauty. Though the congregation liked to criticize and compare their work, the least of them could bring tears to our eyes.

The old men imitated them, praying according to Jewish custom aloud but not in unison, a flamboyant, grotesque howling and muttering, the cantorial dandyism of various parts of Europe aped and distorted. Near the end of the three-hour service they let themselves go wildly in an orgy of competing trills, flourishes, barks and whimpers. Then they crowded the stairs to the basement, where they pressed and pushed around the post-service Sabbath feast of herring, bread, sponge cake, chickpeas and the Seagram's 7 they called "schnapps." Grandpa Dave, in contrast, sometimes showed up in the morning before I left for school, to take me for a day of authorized hooky-playing. He took me to New York for lunch at a good restaurant, and always bought me a new pair of shoes. His capacity for grief did not show. We drove to the city in his Packard, which was the same pearl gray as his hat. The steering wheel was ivory.

III

There were words in Hebrew of which I did learn the meaning, a central part of the liturgy, immensely different from the apocalyptic force of my Haftorah in Isaiah. This opposition has an historical parallel which I can only begin, dimly, to understand.

Apparently, historical Judaism—as long ago as the time of the Essenes and early Christians—turned away from the emphasis upon eschatology, upon a God who created light and darkness, whose New World will efface all memory of the old. In *A History of Religious Ideas,* Mircea Eliade describes the replacement of apocalyptic thought by legal thought, the "glorification of the Torah." Eliade quotes the rabbi who maintained that the existence of the world depended on the fact that Israel accepts Torah. In Eliade's words, "The immutability of the Torah and the triumph of legalism together put an end to eschatological hopes." He quotes Hengel's *Judaism and Hellenism:* "Even apocalyptic literature gradually died out and was replaced by Jewish mysticism." This seems an exaggeration, neglecting Jewish mysticism concerned with final things, from the Essenes to the modern period. But even Gershom Scholem, in *Major Trends of Jewish Mysticism,* speaks of a "lack of apocalyptic elements in the Messianic conception of Hasidism." Scholem also refers, in a tantalizing phrase, to "apocalyptic nostalgia" as a powerful motive force in Merkabah mysticism.

The words I can remember translating are those of the *Shema,* the liturgical cornerstone of daily observance. The *Shema* is a call, not to the apocalypse or the New Jerusalem, but to daily faith. Its main body is Deuteronomy 6:4–9. In the English of the Weekday Prayer Book:

> Hear, O Israel, the Lord our God, the Lord is One. Praised be this glorious sovereignty for ever and ever.

> You shall love the Lord your God with all your heart, with all your soul, and with all your might. These words which I command you this day shall be in your heart. You shall teach them diligently to your children. You shall talk about them at home and abroad, night and day. You shall bind them as a sign upon your hand; they shall be as frontlets between your eyes, and you shall inscribe them on the doorposts of your homes and upon your gates.

The power of this is the verbal power of law. These terms describe the force of the reiterated "all" and "all," the uncompromising "shall," the blanketing pairs "home and abroad," "night and day." But I mean also the exacting, intimate legal force of the document's utterance: *These words which I command you this day.* This is a contract to be honored immediately, not a prophecy to which ears and hearts will be made fat.

I think that to a child with even an eye turned toward the secular world, it demands an impossibility. In contrast, the pathos of God's misplaced care, in Isaiah 5, assumes bad worship, and gives it an emotional place:

> Now I will sing to my well beloved a song of my beloved touching his vineyard. My well beloved hath a vineyard in a very fruitful hill:

> And he fenced it, and gathered out the stones thereof, and planted it with the choicest vine, and built a tower in the midst of it, and also made a winepress therein: and he looked that it should bring forth grapes, and it brought forth wild grapes.

> And now, O inhabitants of Jerusalem, and men of Judah, judge, I pray you, betwixt me and my vineyard.

These lyrical lines are spoken as by one who, stricken with conscience, had his lips cauterized by a live coal, speaking in a transformed and transforming way. The contractual poetry of the *Shema* is like the voice of God, preceding conscience but engendering it. It is a solemn statement of obligation, and the duties it exacts—to love God entirely, constantly, demonstrably—are not exactly impossible. The devout do perform them. But unlike Isaiah's drama of the vineyard, the *Shema* does not admit failure. Isaiah's beloved God expends care, and expects a good harvest, but instead gets wild grapes. Judgment and sorrow will follow; ultimately apocalypse, the one hope, will follow, and the remnant and the New Jerusalem. But the wild grapes have a place in this drama. The *Shema* is immediate: *these words which I command you this day.*

That command engenders not despair, but a kind of shrug, in the less than totally devout. This is a practical matter: one is supposed to pray each day, to bind the literal leather thongs, bearing the black boxes containing sacred words, around one's arm and head while praying. This is a symbol of the mental and verbal devotion that is also a practical matter: *you shall talk about them at home and abroad, night and day.* Such a level of observance, though it omits the role and concept of wild grapes altogether, is bracing, even in a dry way inspiring. It becomes a standard of devotion, saluted and abandoned.

Once one has entertained that harsh standard, a formal or institutional compromise may seem impossible. Our rabbi's frequent sermons denouncing Long Branch's infant, but prosperous, Reform Temple merely re-enforced this feeling. We blew the *shofar;* they kept this ram's horn instrument in a glass case, with a label explaining that their ancestors blew it. I had heard the Reform rabbi, Dr. Tartufkovich, speak at a couple of high school inter-faith assemblies. Maybe I judged him unfairly. In line with my family prejudices, I found him slick, self-satisfied, excessively well fed. He and his family made being Jewish seem easy; if my Bar Mitzvah studies had taught me anything, it was that being Jewish was demanding, and if impossibly demanding—*all your heart and all your soul*—the more matter for pride. The revamping of that stern formal contract, the diluting of the severe expectation of the vineyard, made Rabbi Tartufkovich and his institutional compromise seem not Jewish: less

Jewish than Grandpa Dave, who if he was a "bad Jew" was at least a bad Orthodox Jew.

A more likely compromise is personal. The total demand of the *Shema* is not a power to be fought like an institutional Church, or a power to be denied and fled like the threat of hellfire. It is not the dramatic power of ritual, like the laying on of frontlets itself, nor the poetic power of passages like Isaiah 5's vineyard. It is a verbal power, and therefore one deals with it by interpretation and accommodation. In relation to the legal demands of observance, this seems a shabby, pusillanimous process. But in relation to apocalypse, the immense scale of Isaiah's paradoxical charge, self-definition takes on more dignity, if not validity. To be wild grapes is not to be merely a malfeasor.

To put it simply, I mean the familiar process in which one decides what kind of Jew to be, decides the degree and nature of Jewishness. My father, for example, is a moderate man in most things. A member of the synagogue, he never attended Sabbath services. That is, like many of his friends, he performed a kind of respectable minimum. Partly, this is the mild conformity to custom of a small-town boy; my father worked all his life in the town where he grew up, a celebrated local athlete, voted best-looking boy in his graduating class. His characteristic moderation may also be partly a reaction to growing up in Dave's irregular household. Rose, my father's mother and Dave's first wife, a love-match, died in her twenties. Molly, Dave's second wife, was supplied by Rose's family as a kind of replacement, to care for the two small children. Though she bore Dave two more children, the marriage was not a success. She went insane. At some point, Dave began living partly in a second household with Della Lawyer, the barmaid. When Molly was institutionalized, Della moved in with Dave and the children of both wives and cared for them, but Della and Dave were not married until after my father graduated from high school. In a small town, these matters must have attracted some attention. They might have made a respectable mildness of personal life seem attractive.

I go into this family history because it sheds an interesting light on the questions of worship, observance and idolatry. When Dave Pinsky died, I was twelve, my father was about thirty-five, a hardworking small businessman. It is a remarkable fact that faithfully, for the prescribed eleven months, my father—young, pragmatic, preoccupied with worldly concerns—went to the synagogue daily, to say morning prayers and the *kaddish* for the dead, for his irreligious father, binding the leather *tefilin* around his arms and head. This meant getting up at perhaps six in the morning, in order to get to the synagogue, pray with the old men, and begin the working day that went from eight or eight-thirty until six; until nine on Thursday nights.

Not long ago, I asked my father why he performed this remarkably tedious, prolonged observance: eleven months of early rising and bondage to a ritual that I feel sure was not inspiring or sustaining for him. Did Grandpa Dave have an unsuspected connection to Judaism? Well, no, said my father; you know: he was a tough guy. Had Grandpa Dave been Bar-Mitzvah'ed? My father had no idea. Then why in the world say *kaddish* for him, for eleven months, winter and summer?

"Well, he made me do it with him when my mother died."

My father was a child of seven or eight at the time. Dave's bootlegging activities would have been near their height. There is a sentimental appeal in the picture of the youthful rum-runner, in his sporty clothes, taking his small child with him each weekday morning, for nearly a year, to say memorial prayers for his young wife. For one thing, it is a love story. Thirty years later, my father's observance, in turn, seems to express an attractive, dignified piety toward both parents, perhaps toward the love story, and certainly toward the feelings of the small child, his former self.

But in the strict terms of my Haftorah, Isaiah 66, is any of this in the spirit of acceptable worship? Or is it, rather, idolatry? It is idolatry, because it is autonomously defined: "They have chosen their own ways, and their soul delighteth in their abominations." On the other hand, the Lord whose throne is heaven and footstool the earth finds the flaw in even elaborate worship, the incense that is like blessing an idol, the sacrifice that is like cutting a dog's neck. Only the humble spirit, that trembles at God's word, is not idolatrous. "Humble spirit" does not describe Grandpa Dave as most people saw him. Whether it justly describes the spirit in which he said *kaddish* for his first wife, God knows. We can think that when flesh mourns for flesh—parent or lover—it must be humble, having tasted its own end, in its mourning.

The large, prophetic perspective of Isaiah 66 does offer the idea

—a forgiving idea, in its way, since it is leveling—that all worship, even the most meticulous or elaborate, may be flawed by the spirit of idolatry. Because we have human breath in our nostrils, it is perhaps even likely—or fated—to be flawed. This tragic idea has a comic counterpart in the tendency of Jews to find other Jews either not Jewish enough, or absurdly too Jewish, in their religious practices. If the pious are too sure that their worship is adequate, then perhaps it too is idolatrous. Isaiah himself felt he was "a man of unclean lips," until the seraph touched his lips with the live coal, like a representative particle of the world's end. Such flaws of our "unclean lips" in general can be redeemed only by the actual, unimaginable end of this world, the end foretold in Isaiah 66.

The images associated with this end, at the end of the Book of Isaiah itself, are for the most part terrifying and punitive: "For by fire and by his sword will the Lord plead with all flesh: and the slain of the Lord will be many." Yet the images of the restored Jerusalem are maternal, and the language forges itself into rejoicing:

Rejoice ye with Jerusalem, and be glad with her, all ye that love her: rejoice for joy with her, all ye that mourn for her.

That ye may suck, and be satisfied with the breasts of her consolations; that ye may milk out, and be delighted with the abundance of her glory.

For thus saith the Lord, Behold, I will extend peace to her like a river, and the glory of the Gentiles like a flowing stream; then shall ye suck, ye shall be borne upon her sides, and shall be dandled upon her knees.

As one whom his mother comforteth, so will I comfort you, and ye shall be comforted in Jerusalem.

                                                    Isaiah 66:10–13

At the end of time, when the chosen of God come "out of all nations upon horses, and in chariots, and in litters, and upon mules, and upon swift beasts, to my holy mountain Jerusalem," such comfort will be eternal.

And corruption will be eternal, too. In the final words of the
Book of Isaiah:

> For as the new heavens and the new earth, which I will make, will
> remain before me, saith the Lord, so shall your seed and your name
> remain.
>
> And it shall come to pass, that from one new moon to another, and
> from one Sabbath to another, shall all flesh come to worship before
> me, saith the Lord.
>
> And they shall go forth, and look upon the carcasses of the men that
> have transgressed against me: for their worm shall not die, neither
> shall their fire be quenched; and they shall be an abhorring unto all
> flesh.
>
> Isaiah 66:22–24

The appalling, paradoxical idea of the unending destruction of flesh
supplies a suitable image for the climax of the Book of Isaiah, with
its recurring disasters and admonitions. They are peculiar words for
a child to sing to a watching audience, sealing his admission into
a community of worship he more than half knows he will leave.
The most peculiar thing about the concluding passage for me is also
communal: the eery going forth of the chosen to look upon the
abhorrent, endless process of corruption. It is a ritual, paradoxically
so because time has ended, and a ritual of the flesh, beholding flesh.
Just as the worldly idolators must yield up their powers and plea-
sures, because flesh is doomed to corruption, the poetic power of
Isaiah, calling his deaf audience to transcend the body and its works,
must depend upon images of the maternal, comforting but endlessly
dying body, to speak to our mortal ears.

PS 3566 .I54 P6 1988
Pinsky, Robert.
Poetry and the world